A New Look at Postgraduate Failure

A New Look at Postgraduate Failure

Ernest Rudd

The Society for Research
into Higher Education
& NFER-NELSON

Published by SRHE & NFER-NELSON
At the University, Guildford, Surrey GU2 5XH

First published 1985
© Ernest Rudd

ISBN 1 85059 009 5
Code 8944 02 1

Typeset-and Artwork by FD Graphics, Fleet, Hampshire.
Printed and Bound by Billings & Sons Ltd., Worcester.

Contents

Acknowledgements

I am greatly indebted to a number of people for the help that has made this book possible. Taking them in chronological order, I must acknowledge, first, a grant from the Social Science Research Council (as it then was) and the assistance of the Research Council's staff. Next, I received help, for which I am extremely grateful, from a number of registrars of universities and colleges. They took staff off other work to comb their records for names and addresses and sent out envelopes for me. I am sorry that the need to preserve respondents' anonymity prevents me from thanking them individually.

Without the willingness of my respondents to welcome me into their homes and to their places of work and to talk freely and frankly to me, this research would have been still-born. I am deeply grateful to them for their friendly help; indeed, when leaving them, at the end of an interview, I often felt a regret that a budding friendship would not be continued.

The hospitality of the Swedish National Board for Universities and Colleges (UHÄ) and the Education Department of Uppsala University eased the writing of the concluding chapters, and for this I must thank especially Lennart Levin and Urban Dahlöff.

My chapters were typed, at Essex, by Linda George and Mary Girling, and, at Uppsala, by Berit Fryklund. I am grateful to all of them, but especially to Berit, whose skill in typing in a language not her own astonished me.

I would also like to thank the three friends (John Ashworth, Brian Pippard and Cyril Smith) who read and commented on my draft.

Last but not least I owe a debt of gratitude to Sally Kington for her helpful and constructive suggestions and for the kindly patience and hard work that have turned my manuscript into a book.

Definitions and Terminology

Firstly, where the British speak of 'postgraduate students', the Americans call them 'graduate students'. I prefer this simpler, shorter and more accurate American usage. As, however, there are occasions when it can, in the British context, be ambiguous, I use both terms interchangeably.

Secondly, I try to avoid repetition of the lengthy phrase 'universities, polytechnics and colleges'. To call them collectively 'institutions', as the Swinnerton-Dyer Report does, carries connotations of the Poor Law that are uncomfortably apt. Most postgraduate study, and especially postgraduate research, is at universities; so it does not seem unreasonable to speak of 'universities' where the sense of what I am saying should be taken as applying to polytechnics and other colleges too.

Thirdly, if, in talking about 'the student' or 'the supervisor', I use the pronoun 'he', this does not mean that either person is, or should be, more often male than female — only that I am using a standard convention of the English language rather than the more cumbersome phraseology preferred by feminists today.

1

The Problem

This book is about the reasons why some postgraduate students, especially research students, are not wholly successful in their studies, either failing to gain the degrees at which they were aiming or taking inordinately long to do so. It is therefore principally about the students themselves, but to a certain extent also about the universities and departments in which they were studying, and the teachers with whom they were interacting.

But I will begin by considering

- what is thought to be gained from postgraduate study
- what, if anything is thought to be lost when students delay or do not complete
- what inquiry has been made into the matter to date
- what figures we already have for success (or failure) rates
- what changes have already been made that might be expected to have affected success rates.

First I will sum up what students, staff and society in general appear to gain from postgraduate study, and what is apparently lost when students delay or do not complete it.

GAINS FROM POSTGRADUATE STUDY

The first, and most obvious outcome of postgraduate study is that students learn how to do research. Some skills in this are imparted by most taught courses as well as by study for a research degree.

Secondly, it is frequently claimed that some research students also carry out research that makes a substantial contribution to knowledge and scholarship in a wide range of fields. This was the theme of many of the contributions to the conferences on research and postgraduate study convened between 1981 and 1983 by the SRHE Leverhulme Programme of Study into the Future of Higher Education. Speakers from fields as far apart as history and biology claimed that graduate students contributed not only a substantial proportion of new work in their fields, but also a disproportionate share of the most innovative.

Thirdly, while learning to do research or following taught courses, students acquire (to varying degrees) a range of skills of general applicability.

Students' own listing of these is described in Chapter 9. The most important are probably a greater capacity for critical, constructive and independent thought, the ability to scan and digest written material rapidly, and the ability to write fluently and in a well-organized way.

Fourthly, students learn where their own abilities lie and what careers they want to follow.

Fifthly, some forms of graduate study lead directly to specific careers, for example in certain branches of engineering or management. Less vocational forms of graduate study open the way to some popular careers, which have, at least in the past, had high prestige, such as university teaching and other kinds of scholarly activity and research.

Sixthly, students gain an intellectual and aesthetic satisfaction from graduate study, and especially from research.

And finally, supervisors gain greater satisfaction from the supervision of postgraduate students than from undergraduates, and supervisors, their departments and their universities gain prestige from the numbers of their postgraduate students.

When in later chapters we turn to ways of overcoming the difficulties students meet, we shall in effect be considering whether there is any way in which the totality of gains to the student, to the university and to society can be increased; and, as there is hardly any gain without some corresponding loss, this implies drawing up some kind of calculus for the summation of gains and losses. I can offer no such calculus. However, those whose payment of the piper enables them to call the tune give far more weight to the gains that benefit society that to those that, for example, benefit a university department, and I shall therefore be concentrating on the former. I take them to be, first, the acquisition of useful and needed skills and the opening of a route to a useful career (principally the first and third point mentioned above, but also the fourth and fifth) and, secondly, significant contributions to knowledge (the second point above).

LOSS OR GAIN BY DELAY

To the question of what is lost by failure, with or without delay, has to be added a second, what is lost by delay followed by success. It is about those who, although delayed, do eventually complete their studies that it is most difficult to form any overall judgement whether there is any loss from delay. A number of cases have occurred in the humanities and social sciences where a PhD candidate has taken an exceptionally long time to complete a thesis, but has eventually produced a work of major scholarship, or where he has written a series of significant articles before getting round to writing the thesis. It is sometimes argued that if such students had had to submit their theses more quickly there would have been a serious loss to scholarship.

It is difficult to evaluate this argument, partly due to a high element of subjectivity in it which seems to rate certain single books that took ten years to write as more valuable than the two or three books that others might have written in the same time. Also it would take a major study to discover how often these path-making works are produced by research students who have spent a very substantial time on their thesis, or, which may be more important, what proportion of long-term students produce such major works. I suspect, on scant evidence, that they are not very frequent. It is noticeable that some scholars who put forward this argument have themselves produced a string of publications which started not all that long after they graduated and have continued at short intervals.

What evidence I have on the frequency with which the students who take longer on their theses publish articles and books is distilled in Table 1.1.

It is clear that if productivity is measured by the quantity of published work, those who completed their doctorates quickly were substantially more productive, few of them had no publications at all, and amongst all who had published, they had published the most.

Those who had been relatively slow, taking more than four years, had, in every field, published markedly less. Even amongst those who had not, by 1966, gained their doctorates, who might have been expected to have published virtually nothing, there were many who had some publications — about half the respondents in all fields other than social studies, where they were five-sixths of respondents. However, these figures need to be treated with caution: they are undoubtedly too high because, amongst those who had not yet gained their higher degrees, those who were in occupations that made it likely they would publish were also relatively likely to answer our questionnaire.

What is sure is that amongst the least successful in their attempt at a higher degree there were some who had published, though far fewer of them than amongst the more successful.

The detailed tabulation shows that amongst all groups there are a few highly prolific individuals with outstanding publication records, but, as one would expect, they are very rare amongst those who had not gained their degree, more common amongst the others. On the one hand, those who do not gain their higher degree, or are very slow in gaining it, cannot be written off as complete failures; on the other hand, they are far less likely to become highly productive scholars.

If we are thinking of the hare and the tortoise here, we must remember that many tortoises go to sleep in the sun too.

Berelson (1960) shows a similar pattern in figures for the relationship between the time taken to gain the doctorate and whether recipients of the doctorate had published more than five articles during the previous five years. He comments 'the better people tend to finish sooner and the better people are more productive.'

Any attempt to deal with the question of postgraduate success or failure by concentrating on better initial selection, and having those likely to be very slow or not to gain the higher degree eliminated at the outset, would undoubtedly reduce the total of academic publications a little. Without some information on the extent to which slower workers contribute to those highly innovative advances of knowledge and scholarship that are acknowledged to come from students, it is more difficult to predict the effect on the quantity and quality of publications of any measures to ensure that the slow complete their studies in a shorter time. Perhaps those who would ultimately have produced innovative work but who would instead have been encouraged to produce a shorter quicker thesis, would still proceed to produce the more innovative work later.

My own assessment of the balance of probability here is that such a change might possibly produce some reduction in the output of significant

Table 1.1

Doctoral candidates who entered postgraduate studies in 1957 and who studied full-time or partly full-time, analysed by the time taken to gain the doctorate (up to 1966): composite index of publications.

Time taken to gain doctorate (months)	Percentage with no publications	Percentage publishing thesis in full	Average index of publications* All group	Average index of publications* Those with publications only	Number of respondents** No.	Number of respondents** %
a Technology						
36 or less	5.9	22.9	5.88	6.63	33	22
37-38	16.1	11.5	3.52	4.07	62	41
49 or more	17.1	2.9	2.30	2.81	35	23
Not gained	54.5	0	0.80	1.75	22	15
All respondents	19.6	10.5	3.35	4.14	151	100
b Science						
36 or less	3.7	16.5	6.75	7.02	188	28
37-48	5.6	12.1	5.63	5.97	300	44
49 or more	17.6	16.8	3.61	4.38	131	19
Not gained	48.4	1.6	1.66	3.12	64	9
All respondents	11.4	13.2	5.17	5.84	680	100
c Social Studies						
36 or less	15.4	23.1	13.35	16.69	13	24
37-48	9.1	9.1	9.00	10.13	11	20
49 or more	15.8	10.5	7.33	8.80	19	35
Not gained	16.7	0	5.57	7.12	12	22
All respondents	14.5	10.9	8.59	10.35	55	100
d Language, Literature and Area Studies						
36 or less	0	66.7	22.92	22.92	6	10
37-48	12.5	25.0	6.69	7.64	8	14
49 or more	17.9	21.4	6.78	8.32	28	47
Not gained	47.1	0	2.94	5.88	17	29
All respondents	23.7	20.3	7.39	9.79	59	100
e Other Arts						
48 or less	14.3	28.6	10.29	12.00	7	11
49 or more	23.3	16.7	7.02	8.84	30	48
Not gained	42.3	0	2.64	4.71	26	41
All respondents	30.2	11.1	5.61	7.94	63	100

This table is derived from the detailed and complex information on their publications given by respondents to our survey of 1957 entrants to postgraduate study.

*The index of publications is compiled by counting an article or patent under sole authorship as one unit, either of these under joint authorship as a half unit, a book under sole authorship as five units and a book under joint authorship as two.

**The index of publications is based only on respondents giving full information on these, who were 2.6% fewer.

scholarship in certain branches of the humanities and social sciences, but it would be small in relation to the total output of published research from students.

On the other side of the balance we have to place the potential output of those students who as it is produce nothing because they are trying to do too much, or have not properly planned their work. My guess is that there are enough such cases for there to be a substantial gain to scholarship if the way some students did their research were improved.

Would there be a loss if a change took place that simply cut out slow students? That would depend on whether whatever they did instead of research were more valuable than the lost scholarly output. Some academics tend at times to talk as if they believed that nothing could ever compensate for any loss of scholarship. I am not sure that they really believe this; I am quite sure that virtually no one outside the universities does.

The tragedy at present is that we are losing from many students both the results that ought to come out of their research and the results of whatever alternative work they might be doing. This is part of the case for change.

ALTERNATIVE WAYS OF ACQUIRING WIDER SKILLS

Let us now turn to graduate students' acquisition of skills other than at research — those of general applicability. Here again we have to consider two questions: what would be lost or gained by students completing a thesis more rapidly and successfully; and what would be lost or gained if they had never started postgraduate studies at all.

I discuss in Chapter 7 what students lose from their failure to write up their research — the most frequent point of failure. All the stages of research are important, from the choice of a topic and the initial reading and planning to the writing of an account of it all — what has been done and why, what has been found out, and how these results fit into the general body of knowledge. To omit any stage is to lose much education in skills of general applicability. This is broadly the point of view put forward also by the Swinnerton-Dyer Committee (ABRC 1982), whose work I describe more fully below.

But what of the other question — whether the more dilatory students and those who are not going to be successful in research or a taught course with a substantial research element should enter that kind of postgraduate study at all? The loss to them, to their future employers (and perhaps to other indirect beneficiaries, such as the community at large) would then be the skills and experience they would have gained in postgraduate study up to the point at which they gave it up; but on the other side of the balance sheet would be the gain of whatever skills and experience they would have received in whatever alternative occupation they would have followed.

Included in experience is their clearer understanding of what kinds of work they can, or cannot, do and enjoy. As research students they have had the opportunity to gain this understanding of their suitability for research and for some of the other kinds of work they have met — notably computing. But in a job outside higher education they would have made comparable discoveries; and, as they might have held more than one job in the time that they spent as postgraduate students, there is a slight balance in favour of the outside job.

The best way to weigh the skills gained in postgraduate study against those they might have gained elsewhere is by their market value − what employers are willing to pay for them. Other kinds of assessment, such as by the views of whoever within a firm happens to be answering a survey questionnaire, are less reliable.

The Department of Employment study of the careers of 1970 graduates (Williamson 1981) was able to compare the earnings in 1977 of those with doctorates, with masters and with no postgraduate qualification. For men this comparison is made for five groups of subjects, six groups of occupations, seven types of work and seven sectors of employment. In all but three of these twenty-five comparisons the graduates with PhDs were paid less than those with no postgraduate qualification; the exceptions were those employed in scientific research, in polytechnics, and in a group described as 'other education', which is broadly schools and further education colleges. Earnings in scientific research were substantially below the overall average, and even within research the holders of doctorates were paid only 3.8 per cent more than those without a postgraduate qualification. The respondents without a PhD employed in the universities were paid more than those with one.

The value employers set on a masters degree is less clear cut. Generally, respondents with a masters earned more than those with doctorates, and less than those with no higher degree, but there were a number of exceptions. In particular, certain masters degrees in engineering and in management studies seemed to bring increased incomes.

A multiple regression analysis showed that, whereas each year of work experience had added £275 to graduates' salaries, each year of postgraduate study had added only £70.

Regrettably the Swinnerton-Dyer Working Party in some parts of their report (ABRC 1982) seem to have misunderstood these figures and other related data. In their concluding chapter they offer two explanations. One is that 'among graduates with good degrees the characteristics that incline someone to go into postgraduate work may well be ones that would make that person relatively less attractive to potential non-academic employers'. This is something which it is difficult to prove or disprove. However, a number of studies carried out at various times have shown that graduates with first class honours degrees, of whom a substantial proportion from amongst the 1970 graduates went into postgraduate education, have commanded a higher salary than graduates with seconds, who, in their turn earned more than other graduates. For example, a 1954 study of 1950 graduates (PEP 1956) − made at a time when many graduates were going straight into employment who would, if they had graduated in later years, have gone into postgraduate study − found that the median salary for a graduate with a first was £708, with a second £680 and with neither £669.

It would be more reasonable to conclude from such figures that the people who went into postgraduate study, having better than average degrees, would have been the more attractive, not the less attractive to an employer.

Secondly, the Swinnerton-Dyer Working Party in the descriptive section of their report say, with reasonable accuracy: 'Part of the reason for the low earnings of PhDs is that they are concentrated in occupations that are generally low-paying (by graduate standards)'. However, when they turn to analysis and recommendations, they say something rather different: 'The obvious reason for this is that those who take a PhD are more likely than other graduates to enter a low-paid profession – in particular, to pursue an academic career'. This begs the question of whether it is an over-production of graduates with higher degrees, and especially doctorates, that has made the professions that employ them relatively low-paid. But, leaving that on one side, this reasoning ignores the nature of the multiple regression analysis, where the graduates' occupations were one of the variables used in the equations. So the lower earnings of holders of doctorates are found even after all allowance has been made for their different distribution between occupations.

There can be no reasonable doubt whatsoever that, in most cases, postgraduate study reduces graduates' earnings in the early years of their careers and turns them from the kinds of graduates employers want to the kinds they want less. The main exceptions are graduates who have followed certain highly vocational taught courses. The Swinnerton-Dyer Working Party pointed out that one cannot from these data come to any conclusion about earnings later in the career. However, the Department of Employment figures are not for starting salaries but for salaries when a few years into a career; and so one might ask, in return, what kind of useful qualification produces extra earnings (if at all) only when its holder has gone so far from receiving it that his salary is, in any case, determined almost entirely by his experience and achievements in a job, and by his personal qualities?

One implication of this is that those postgraduate students who were more than usually dilatory or were unsuccessful in their research would almost certainly have gained higher incomes, and been regarded by employers as more valuable, if they had never entered postgraduate study at all.

Against this it is often argued that there is another kind of need for graduates trained to do research – a need of which employers are unaware. It is argued that employers do not know that it is in their best interests, and that they and the economy would benefit if they employed more graduates trained for research.

There are many counter-arguments to this somewhat arrogant stance: for example, that Britain needs to improve not its research but its use of research, and that giving industry more of the brighter graduates with first degrees, and then up-dating them on scientific advances by very short courses lasting only a few days each might be the way to bring this about. Also that one cannot reform industry by flooding it with graduates of a kind it does not want – all that produces is discontented graduates.

Britain is not alone in having apparently overproduced PhDs. The USA may not have had the problem longer, but has at least shown greater awareness of it – see for example Cartter (1976). Indeed, one group of authors has produced a book significantly entitled *Underemployed PhDs* and devoted it to the thesis that, although few graduate students can possibly get the jobs to which they hope their PhDs will lead, there are other interesting jobs they could take (Solmon, Kent, Ochsner and Hurwicz 1981).

This, then, is the wider gackground to the delay and dropping out that I describe below. It cannot be accepted as axiomatic that an increase in the numbers of postgraduate students benefits both the students and society. On the contrary it can be said with some confidence that any change that reduced the number of postgraduate students would benefit employers and the economy. It would probably also, on balance, benefit the potential students. But it would reduce somewhat the output of research results and scholarship.

EARLIER RESEARCH

It is a constant plaint that too little research is done into higher education. And of that research that is done, any that makes a useful contribution to knowledge about postgraduate study is especially sparse — or at least that is true of what is published in the English language and easily available in Britain. (For a brief survey of the published research see Rudd (1984).)

The pioneering research was by Berelson (1960) who covered the whole subject of graduate education very widely, drawing on surveys of recent recipients of the doctorate, and of teaching staff and graduate deans.

Next came the aptly named *Stipends and Spouses* by Davis (1962), which related the very considerable length of time often taken over the doctorate in the USA to the students' need to support themselves through research assistantships, teaching assistantships, and often their wives' earnings. More recent researchers looking at graduate students in the USA have, however, tended to concentrate largely on one facet of the composition of the student body — the relative under-representation of women and of certain minority ethnic groups.

The only more recent major work in the USA that has dealt to any substantial extent with postgraduate students' problems, and with the processes of change that their postgraduate education is intended to bring about, is by Katz and Hartnett (1976). This is a symposium volume, consisting of a series of loosely related chapters by authors who have been associated together in research. The subjects they cover include recruitment into graduate study, the kind of environment for learning that is provided and the students' reaction to it, the meaning of quality, and various personal and study problems the students have.

In Britain, apart from the work of my own research group (Rudd and Hatch 1968; Rudd 1975), and the surveys carried out by the Policy Studies Institute for the Swinnerton-Dyer Working Party, to which I refer below, there have been two other substantial pieces of research (Glennerster 1966; and Welsh 1978, 1979, 1980, 1981) and these have concentrated entirely on the researcher's own institution. An advantage Welsh gained from studying her own university (Aberdeen) was that it enabled her to interview both the students and their supervisors and to compare what they said in a way that would not have been feasible for an outsider. Her study is especially valuable for this reason, and I shall be making use of her findings here.

THE SWINNERTON-DYER WORKING PARTY

In 1979, the Advisory Board for the Research Councils felt it necessary to review the policies of the research councils for the provision of postgraduate training and the extent to which they were meeting Britain's needs for trained manpower. The part of the Working Party's terms of reference most closely related to the subject of my research instructed it to:

(iv) consider whether present arrangements secure postgraduates of the requisite quality and background and provide them with the appropriate training.

The Working Party began by soliciting the views of a wide range of organizations, arranging for the collection of fresh data on completion rates in postgraduate study and the analysis of existing data (to which I return below) and commissioning two surveys by the Policy Studies Institute (Brown 1982; Whalley 1982). I have discussed elsewhere (Rudd 1983) those considerable weaknesses of these surveys that greatly reduce their value.

I made available to the Working Party some preliminary results of my own research that were relevant to specific issues about which I had heard they were interested, and also put forward my early thoughts on the policy issues.

They discussed my evidence and suggestions in their report (ABRC 1982), and I, in turn, discuss some of their conclusions and recommendations principally in Chapter 11.

THE STATISTICS

The first attempt made to collect overall national figures for success and failure in postgraduate study (Rudd and Hatch 1968) related to students who entered postgraduate study in 1957. All the universities (except Oxford, Cambridge and Battersea Polytechnic/University of Surrey) supplied information on everyone who became an internal postgraduate student in that year. Information direct from the students as well as from other sources indicated that the omission of the three universities made little difference to the overall percentages achieving their degrees.

In 1957 few universities limited the length of time for which a student could be registered for a research degree, which produced a conceptual problem. Whereas one could say of undergraduates that, after a given period, all those who had not gained their degrees had failed or had given up their studies, there was an additional category at postgraduate level which could not be described as having succeeded or failed or given up – those who were still plodding on long after they started their studies, or who at least had stayed on the books of their universities as still intending to complete. Therefore the figures we collected for the numbers who had achieved, by 1966, the degrees which they set out to gain some nine years earlier, would not represent the full total. Nevertheless, nine years is a long time, and there was a basic assumption that all who were going to had indeed gained their degrees by then.

Our figures included, as well as full-time students, a small number, probably a little over a sixth of the total, who were part-time. The part-timers take longer over the degree and are less likely to succeed in gaining it. The inclusion of these students cannot, however, account for more than a small part of the surprisingly high percentage who had not yet gained their degrees – ranging from 10 per cent of diploma students in social studies to 54 per cent of masters students, again in social studies. Technology and science had rather better than average success rates, with 78 per cent and 75 per cent of students, respectively, succeeding, and social studies and arts had rather worse ones – 67 per cent and 51 per cent. At that period many research students in the arts and social studies who today would be working for PhDs were registered for masters degrees by research, while many taught courses which today would lead to masters degrees then led to various diplomas, certificates, etc. On this account alone, therefore, one would expect the success rate today from the PhD to be below the 78 per cent we recorded, while the masters degrees would achieve a better rate than our 54 per cent, since we recorded a success rate of 83 per cent on diploma courses, etc. It must be remembered that those who entered postgraduate study, and especially research, were select graduates: more than half of them having first or upper second class honours degrees — classes of degree gained by no more than a quarter of all graduates.

Surprisingly, there has been no comparable further study of an entire cohort since then, but there have been, in recent years, a few studies which have given some indication of the scale of success, or non-success, in postgraduate study.

The Department of Employment (Williamson 1981) made a postal survey in 1977 of a sample of graduates who had gained first degrees in 1970. Some of these had gone on to postgraduate study, probably most, but not all, in 1970. As their response rate was only a little over a half, and as those who have been less successful are also less likely to answer a questionnaire of this kind, the DE figures for successful completion of a higher degree should be taken as overestimating the true percentage. Of those who attempted a doctorate, 60.5 per cent had succeeded in gaining it. For a masters the figure was 83.4 per cent. The success rate for the two groups combined was 73 per cent.

For comparison, of our 1966 respondents (with a higher response rate) some 81 per cent of doctoral students and some 69 per cent of masters students were successful by the end of seven years, with an overall average for both groups of about 76 per cent — which figures differ from those given above for all graduate students entering in 1957 partly due to bias produced by over 70 per cent of successful candidates but under 50 per cent of the unsuccessful replying, and partly because they show the position after seven years, whereas our survey took place after nine years.

The Swinnerton-Dyer Working Party on Postgraduate Education (ABRC 1982) stimulated the two main research councils to collect data on the completion rates of the postgraduate students they support, the first of these data being collected to help the Working Party's deliberations. The Social Science Research Council (SSRC) found that, of the students who began research in 1973, some 40 per cent had completed it successfully by 1980. The Science and Engineering Research Council (SERC) took a slightly shorter period, from 1974 to 1980, and found that 57 per cent of their research students had gained their PhDs.

One of the recommendations of the Working Party was that the research councils 'should routinely maintain and publish statistics of submission rates for PhD students whom they support', and both the main research councils now do this. It should be noted that, as some students who submit theses do not gain their degrees, figures for submission rates are not comparable with those for completion rates. Their figures for students who began their research in October 1979 (SERC 1984; and ESRC 1984a) have shown that 47.8 of the SERC students had submitted theses by October 1983, compared with 24.9 per cent of the students given awards by the SSRC (now renamed the Economic and Social Research Council).

The figures of both the research councils show a similar pattern — that those universities and university colleges given relatively large numbers of awards, who were mainly, of course, the larger universities, had higher submission rates than those who were given fewer. There were 19 institutions given 40 or more awards by the SERC, and between them they had 62 per cent of the awards. Their submission rate was 51.1 per cent, compared with 45.9 per cent for the 42 university institutions given fewer awards each. The submission rate for the polytechnics was 24.5 per cent.

The ESRC figures show 23 universities and university colleges receiving 10 or more awards and 42 receiving fewer. Those getting the larger numbers of awards accounted for 72 per cent of the total going to the universities and had a completion rate of 24.5 per cent, compared with 18.9 per cent for those institutions having fewer.

These figures cannot be the result of the new policy of giving awards selectively to those institutions with relatively good completion rates; these students received their awards long before this policy was adopted.

The Department of Education and Science, too, has produced figures for the completion rates of its research students in the arts, but has allowed them a longer period, from 1972 to 1982, in which to gain their degrees. They found that 58 per cent of doctoral students and 53 per cent of masters students had gained their degrees.

These surveys are confined to the holders of the main government studentships, who have to hold good honours degrees, and one would expect such students, with adequate, though perhaps not generous financial support, to have higher success rates than students struggling to support themselves from other sources.

Donald Bligh (Bligh 1981) has published an analysis of (otherwise unpublished) Universities Statistical Record figures for full-time research students completing their studies in 1977-79. These figures show rather higher success rates — 82 per cent for doctorates and 57 per cent for masters by research. In their coverage these figures are substantially different from those based on an entry cohort.

What do all these figures tell us? They certainly do not tell us conclusively that completion rates have improved over the years since 1957. Apart from Bligh's figures, which are out of line with the other figures due to differences in coverage, they show that the percentage of entrants to postgraduate study who do not successfully complete their studies is high, and they strongly suggest that, at the point at which the Swinnerton-Dyer Working Party was collecting together its figures, it was rising.

As a whole, the statistics also tell us that in science and technology students gain their doctorates more quickly than in the humanities and social sciences and are more likely to be successful eventually — these two facts are not unrelated.

CHANGES IN FACTORS AFFECTING SUCCESS RATES

Over the period spanned by these figures various changes have occurred that might be expected to affect completion rates. In particular, the number of grants for postgraduate study from central government funds increased more than eight-fold. Amongst our 1957 entry there was a high percentage struggling to manage on various precarious or inadequate sources of finance. This was especially true of the masters students, most of whom were in the arts and social studies, where there were very few central government awards — most of the doctoral students were in science, which was more generously supported. Lack of money can be a spur to completing a thesis quickly, but it is more likely to result in the student giving up altogether.

There may well have been one other important and relevant change over the years. It is possible, indeed likely, that the standard of performance expected of the successful PhD candidate has risen. Obviously, there can never be any clear, objective standard for a PhD — every thesis has to be different from any that has come before. Examiners carry in their heads some notion of what the PhD student should have achieved, but this cannot, by the nature of things, be very precise, so that the individual examiner's judgement must vary from time to time — this has, after all, been found to happen when the examiner has the far easier task of evaluating a series of scripts answering the same question paper. That different individual examiners would reach different decisions on marginal cases is even more certain. Nevertheless, for the system to operate at all requires some broad general consensus on what is to be expected for a PhD, and one can assume that such a consensus exists. The question is whether the level, or more likely the broad band of levels, agreed by that consensus has changed from one period to another?

One indication that such a change has taken place is the increase in length of time that a student is expected to take over a PhD. When the PhD was first introduced the grants for research students given by the recently founded Department of Scientific and Industrial Research — the ancestor of a number of the research councils — lasted one year, with the student finding support elsewhere for part or the whole of another year to complete the degree. Then awards began to be given, first occasionally, then more regularly, for a second year, but no more — the ordinary student was expected to complete the PhD in two years. In the thirties, part of a third year would be allowed if at all, only in the most exceptional circumstances, and such extensions did not become a regular part of the students' grant scheme until after the 1939-45 war. The percentage of students asking for a third year gradually rose, but even in the early sixties it was not assumed that every student needed the third year, and an appreciable proportion of PhD students left their universities after two years. However, pressure for occasional extensions for a fourth year was then already beginning, and was very similar to earlier pressure for a second and then a third year.

Of the doctoral candidates who replied to our survey of 1957 entrants, about a quarter of those in science, technology and the social sciences gained their doctorates in 36 months or less — including the time between the writing of the thesis and the examiners' decision. There are strong indications that the percentage gaining the degree in three years would be far smaller today.

One other indication of the standard of the thesis is its length. I am not, of course, implying that a longer thesis is in any way better than a shorter one, only that it takes longer to write, though one might also claim that, other things being equal, the longer thesis represents a higher standard of achievement; however, that conclusion follows largely from other assumptions hidden in the *ceteris paribus* assumption. An indication that the length of the PhD thesis was rising is the decision of many universities in the sixties and seventies to limit its size.

To look into this further, I discussed with Cambridge University Library the possibility of measuring the lengths of a sample of theses. It was not possible to do this, but I was shown the stacks of successful theses arranged by their date. I then realized that the growth in size of theses from the twenties to the time in the mid-sixties when limits on the length were imposed was so conspicuous — one might almost say dramatic — that no elaborate scheme to sample and measure them was needed.

The reason for this increase in the length of theses and the time taken to complete them cannot be more than speculation. One obvious explanation is that, as knowledge is growing exponentially, the amount that has to be included in the literature survey is also growing. This seems to me a somewhat superficial explanation. As knowledge grows so the field of knowledge fragments into smaller and smaller areas, which ought to push the trend in the opposite direction. Moreover, there is no fixed limit to what has to be included in the survey of the literature. All of knowledge is interrelated, so one could make an argument for the impossible task of including everything. The decision at what point, short of the totality of knowledge, to stop must be arbitrary.

Similarly it can be argued that, as knowledge grows, more work is needed to cross its frontier. I find this, too, unconvincing. On the frontier there are still small, medium-sized and big research topics. So students and their supervisors have a choice, and one would expect them to choose a topic that is at least a little bigger than the minimum below which the topic would be too small for a PhD.

It seems to me more likely that the perception of supervisors and examiners of the level of achievement that merits a PhD is changing, and one should look for some built-in mechanism that results in a gradual rise in these perceptions. One such mechanism could be supervisors and examiners seeing those theses that have passed, including their own, as staking out the level of the PhD. A successful thesis has to go over that level, and it is then, in its turn, seen as staking out a very slightly higher level.

The imposition of a limit to the length of the thesis would have little effect on such a process. The maximum permitted length is irrelevant to most scientists — whose theses are, in any case, brief — and in other fields it may have resulted in students spending even longer writing their theses, because of the need to slim them down to keep them within the maximum without reducing the scope, content or level.

In Sweden an attempt has been made to deal with the time taken to write a thesis by allowing government funds to pay for the printing of the thesis only up to a set limit, with the candidate himself paying for the printing of extra pages; but there are signs that this has not proved wholly effective.

Whatever the mechanism of growth, however, it seems likely that rising expectations of the level of the PhD have produced a rise in that level, which, in its turn, has reduced success rates at a period when the easier availability of studentships should have led to their rising.

THIS STUDY

In our 1966 survey, we asked ex-students who had not obtained the qualification for which they registered to 'give an account of the circumstances which caused you not to obtain the qualification'. We reported the results as follows:

This is not a searching question, and as one might have expected many of the answers were somewhat terse and not particularly illuminating. Some just said 'lost interest' or 'did not complete thesis'. Answers of this kind really beg more questions than they answer. To obtain satisfactory explanations of failure it would have been necessary to carry out a series of thorough interviews.

The intention of this present study was to do just that.

Here I describe the study; give an account of why the people I interviewed had taken so long over their higher degree work, or dropped out from their studies; discuss what they told me; and put forward some policy proposals.

2

The Scope of the Study

RESPONSE AND NON-RESPONSE

I interviewed for this study altogether a little over a hundred people who had registered for a higher degree at one of the thirteen universities and colleges that either sent out letters for me or, in two cases, gave me names and addresses. The universities and colleges covered a broad spectrum, including old, new, and technological, large and small, London, Oxbridge and provincial. There were no universities or colleges in Scotland or Wales in the study; but in earlier research I have not found any specific Welsh or Scottish element in the way they deal with postgraduate students. In an account of her research into postgraduate study at Aberdeen, Jennifer Welsh has noted parallels with my earlier findings (Welsh 1979 and 1980(b); Rudd 1975), and hers could easily be an account of virtually any other university in Britain.

I asked the thirteen universities and colleges to select for me a sample of home (ie British resident) students who had withdrawn fairly recently from postgraduate study, or had tried to gain a degree and failed, or were still registered but had taken an inordinately long time over their studies. My letter to them explained the purpose of my study and asked the recipient to complete a form saying whether he or she was willing to be interviewed. In all, 126 people said they were willing to be interviewed, and 18 that they were unwilling. Another 18 letters were returned by the Post Office or by the occupants of the house to which the letter had been sent.

The interviews started at the end of 1978 and were carried out over the next two years, the journeys around Britain being combined with visits needed for two different research contracts.

Unfortunately, it was not possible to keep track of the numbers of envelopes sent out for me by universities, but there is no doubt that substantial numbers of people either did not receive the letters or, having received them, did not reply at all. Had I intended to produce valid statistics from this survey, the high non-response would have reduced the reliability of the findings. However, this was a different kind of survey, and it was not my aim to discover, for example, what percentage of postgraduate drop-outs are mature students. Instead, I was trying to take a substantial number of individual case-studies, and I was looking for qualitative not quantitative results, so I was not concerned that I might have too few of one kind of case and too many of others. What would be a matter of concern would be if any significant kind of drop-out, dilatory student or failure were totally missing from my respondents. It is therefore worth considering what kind of students or ex-students would be unwilling to talk to me or would be missed for any other reason.

The kinds of people who would be relatively unwilling to be interviewed could be expected to be those who:

a having been very unhappy while postgraduate students would be reluctant to talk about their experiences, or
b were deeply ashamed of their failure, or
c for other reasons wanted to forget the whole experience, or
d believed they did not have anything of interest to tell me.

I may have had disproportionately few respondents in the first category; the overwhelming majority of the people I saw had enjoyed their years as postgraduate students, and I was surprised at the number who, after an account of a series of personal and academic disasters, said that all in all it was a wonderful experience which they were glad they had not missed. But what is important in this context is that I did have a certain number from both groups a and b.

Category c is different. There may well have been students who wanted to forget the whole thing as a result of experiences that differed from any I had met, and I cannot tell what those experiences were; but I can at least be reasonably confident that they would have been more traumatic than those of the students I interviewed, which is itself of some significance, because it suggests that I have not in their cases overstated the nature of the problems I was studying.

I interviewed some like my category d; respondents who were willing to be interviewed although they felt they had little to tell me, and who, indeed, were relatively straightforward cases.

Four of the 18 refusals gave reasons or comments. One said: 'I gave up my part-time MSc course because of increasing job commitments and increasing family responsibilities (ie a new baby!)'. The second said: 'I am too disillusioned about the standard of training given to postgraduate students to wish to grant an oral discussion.' The remaining two were working overseas.

Where letters failed to reach the people to whom they were addressed, it appears in some cases to have been due to copying errors in the addressing, but in most cases resulted from the student moving home without making adequate provision for his mail to be forwarded. It seems likely that those ex-students who did not receive their letters were the more mobile, changing their addresses more frequently, being more rootless, not having the kind of contact with their old addresses that would lead to their mail being forwarded. However, a number of those who answered and were interviewed had been fairly mobile, and had to be traced in various complicated ways.

On the whole, though I cannot know what sorts of cases I missed, the extent of the range of those I interviewed has persuaded me that I am unlikely, through non-response or non-contact, to have missed any that would have added greatly to my knowledge of the reasons for dropping out and failure at postgraduate level.

One feature of my sample that may reflect some kind of selectivity was the substantial number of unclassifiable mavericks. Most were so individual that I can say little about them without a breach of confidence, so four examples must suffice. Two (who were entirely separate) had, when doing a project for a first degree in engineering, produced patentable inventions that had been taken up and used by industry. Another, who had a number of achievements to his credit before he became a very mature student, had recently been featured in advertisements as recommending a certain brand of high quality equipment for the reproduction of music. The advertisement included a photograph, but no explanation of who he was, assuming the reader already knew.

The career of another rather unusual case is exemplified by this extract from the interview – an account of how he first came to enter university, twenty years earlier, after spending a year at a teachers' training college:

> I went home one afternoon and my mother said 'There's a history lecture on in the nearest market town, would you like to go to that and then go back to college?' I said, 'Yes, fine'. I went to this history lecture, got a lift back to the nearest town to my college with the lecturer, who, for many reasons I won't go into, felt I ought to go to university and got me in, ten days later into his own. So I'm the only person I know who went to university without ever having applied.
>
> ER. That was quite something. You were getting an informal interview, in effect, in the car.
>
> Well, I was trying to convert him to the Beethoven later quartets; and he told me, years later, that at the end of the lecture I got up to ask some questions, like the precocious little brat that I was, and I'd apparently neatly revealed an inherent self-contradiction that had been running throughout the whole of his lecture, and he thought, 'How the bloody hell do I get out of this?' And he'd thought anybody who was bright enough to pick that up ought to be at university, and I wasn't.

Again, in this qualitative, but basically unquantitative study, such unrepresentativeness seems, if anything, to be a positive advantage.

THE SHAPE OF THE STUDY: THE INTERVIEW

I initially tried to confine my interviewing to areas where I could do it with the greatest convenience – London, the Home Counties, East Anglia, North Yorkshire, and around Edinburgh. However, this proved impossible because respondents had moved around very widely, and the interviews were eventually confined only within an area east of a line between Brighton, Chester, and Stirling. Altogether 18 respondents who said they were willing to see me were not interviewed because their addresses were too widely scattered, or they had moved home and I lost contact with them, or it was not possible to find a time for the interview that suited both of us, or they had died. One other respondent was included in my list in error, having gained his one-year masters in a year.

The interviews almost all took place at the respondent's home or place of work, and generally lasted a little under an hour. They were tape-recorded and the recordings were subsequently transcribed.

There was no set questionnaire used, though there were, of course, certain topics that I tried to cover with each respondent. In general, after the first one or two questions, most further questions followed from whatever the respondent had just said. As an interviewer, I tried to say as little as possible, leaving the respondent to talk about his experience of postgraduate study with minimal prompting and steering from me. I hope I maintained, and showed, the same friendly and sympathetic interest when being told by one respondent that, since her conversion to women's lib, she had realized how trivial, superficial and useless her research topic was, and by another that, since she became disenchanted with women's lib, she had realized that her research topic was trivial, superficial and useless, or by one student that social studies departments in universities were dominated by the extreme left, and by another that because he held left-wing views he could not get a job in any university department of his branch of social studies.

Knowing I would eventually have to summarize what the student had told me, from time to time I produced on the spot a summary of what had been said and asked if it was fair and accurate. This gave an opportunity to correct any misunderstandings. It was reassuring that it was almost always agreed that my summary was fair and accurate.

The nature of the main areas covered will, I hope, become clear below. In addition to the kind of facts, comments, views, and so on, that I sought, respondents gave me a certain amount of background information that was needed to understand the rest, for example most gave me a detailed account of their research topic.

THE VALIDITY OF THE FINDINGS

I once made an analysis of the road accident files of a major insurance company. When both drivers were insured with the company, I had before me both accounts of the accident, which differed so much in virtually every detail that it was often difficult to believe they were describing the same place and the same events. Many of the students I interviewed had been through what might be described as a three-year smash-up, and although one might expect their account of it to be less biased than that of a motorist, because, whereas many of the motorists were blatantly lying, the students had nothing to gain from lying to me, nevertheless one could not expect them to be wholly detached about it.

Ideally, I would like to have received a frank account from everyone concerned with the circumstances into which I was inquiring, including supervisors, as well as the opportunity to question informants on points where their accounts were at variance. However, to persuade respondents to talk freely I had to assure them that I would treat what they told me as confidential, and that precluded any attempt at cross-checking with the supervisor, or other members of the same department, on whom they were dependent for references when applying for jobs. Therefore, I could see no way of achieving this without behaviour that I would regard as unethical.

Nevertheless, there were many other ways of checking what was said. First, I tried to be alert for self-contradictions and inconsistencies in what I was told, and to explore these more fully with the respondent. Secondly, I was able at times to suggest alternatives to the explanations put forward, which stimulated careful reconsideration of the position the respondent was adopting. This would produce either a modification of what was being said, or a fuller, more circumstantial restatement of it.

Some of the self-contradictions were related, as one would expect, to the blame for their failures that students attached to others; but not all were. A student who repeatedly attributed his failures to his laziness had published more from the results of his three years than almost anyone else I saw.

Thirdly, I was bringing to the accounts I was hearing a fairly substantial knowledge of universities and especially of postgraduate study. This research is only the latest in a series of pieces of research on postgraduate students that I have done over many years. I have also accumulated a fair stock of more anecdotal evidence from various sources, including members of my family, other relations, and friends who have been postgraduate students. I have even dropped out from part-time postgraduate study myself, but for a different reason from any I met during this study – on seeing my first published article my supervisor said that with such publications I had no need of a masters degree. Also, although I have never been a research student, having taken advantage of the arrangement by which London graduates could submit a PhD thesis for examination without being a student at a university or college, or supervised in any other way, I have had the experience of writing a thesis in my spare time while holding a demanding job and needing to find time for my family – conditions which many of the students I interviewed said made the writing of a thesis impossible.

Fourthly, I sometimes knew, personally or by repute, people to whom the students referred, and I never found the comments made on them unfair.

Fifthly, I have, I hope, an academic's facility for seeing that there are many sides to a problem. For example, when a student complained that, after many years of commenting on successive drafts, his supervisor was showing a grave dereliction of duty by taking a month to read and comment on a ninth draft of a chapter, it was easy to see there was another side to the story.

Sixthly, like most people, I was influenced a little in my interpretation by the various small clues that virtually everyone gives to the reliability of his evidence. What is said by someone who exudes the fullest and most unquestioning confidence in his own merits is bound to be interpreted differently from the comments of the more modest. When someone shows very clear signs of psychiatric disturbance, this, too, is bound to affect the reliance one places on his evidence.

Seventhly, students' stories could, to a certain extent, be checked against those of other students, and I generally found that these checks confirmed the impression I had already formed. For example, I formed the opinion that a student's account of getting virtually no teaching or help of any kind during a one-year MA course was likely to reflect her other problems rather more than the teaching that was provided; then later I saw another student from the same course, whose very different account of it supported my view. Altogether, these cross-checks were very valuable. When a student from a department of the highest international repute told me that many of his contemporaries presented theses which represented to a substantial extent the work of their supervisors, I might have dismissed this as the unsuccessful competitor shouting 'foul play' had not another student, who was himself working elsewhere, but whose wife was a secretary in this department, told me that large sections of the theses she was given to type were in the handwriting of the supervisors. Students who told me that, due to the way their research group was run, few of their group succeeded in gaining their PhDs were unlikely to have known I was seeing, and getting the same story from, others from that group. That these stories checked so well gave me greater confidence in those stories I could not cross-check but that had the ring of truth about them.

CONFIDENTIALITY

The undertaking I gave to respondents, that what they told me would not be published in any form from which individuals could be identified, has affected in two ways my reporting of the results of the interviews. First I have had to find some way of disguising individuals that does not distort the relevant facts but does not allow the knowledgeable reader to break my code. I have done this by concealing the names of the universities and making a variety of minor alterations to irrelevant details. Where the sex of the student has no relevance to the story it may (or may not) be changed; and similarly the student's subject, topic or field of study may be changed to one that in all relevant characteristics is very like the actual one. I have not, of course, done this when I am referring to more than one student, or where there is no risk of a student being identified.

Secondly, it has been impossible to put together complete stories that would not be easily identifiable. This is a more serious loss as the circumstances in which the students gave up or failed were rarely so simple as they were liable to appear when individual causes were isolated for discussion; but the full complexity cannot be adequately presented without examples.

Sometimes the same student may appear in more than one guise – as a man in one place and a woman elsewhere, or first as a mediaeval historian and later as a modern historian – especially where the details that can be safely altered without distorting the facts are different in the two places. Any respondent who thinks he recognizes himself has probably found an adapted version of someone else.

THE EDITING OF THE MATERIAL

Spoken English is very different from what is written. People rarely speak in well formed sentences; they often repeat themselves; they invert the order of words; they start a sentence, change their minds, and say something different, sometimes without going back to the beginning. When we hear them we filter out these aberrations, but they show strongly in a transcript. Wholly unedited extracts would sometimes be difficult to read, while, on the other hand, a text that was edited into smoothly flowing prose would, in a way, be untrue to its origins. I have tried to compromise by doing only some basic editing – for example, taking out the words of slight hesitation, 'you know', etc., the repetitions, and the obvious slips of the tongue – while still keeping the quotation as far as possible intact. I have also make minor alterations – eg to the names of people and universities – to protect anonymity here too.

Most of the problems and difficulties that postgraduate students meet occur in a general way across all subjects and fields of study, though in detail they differ not merely from one subject to another but between different research topics within a subject. Therefore, very often, when I quote from students' comments or refer to individual cases, as the student's field of research is irrelevant, I do not mention it. Where it is relevant, this information is given.

Similarly it is not always relevant whether the student was working for a masters degree or a doctorate. There is no sharp dividing line between the two — both generally included elements of courses and research. The failures of the masters students were mainly centred on their research projects, and the problems they met in their research were not greatly different from those met by the doctoral students, even though the scale was different. Even undergraduates carrying out small research projects to be written up as a dissertation meet some of the same problems. Therefore, I only separately distinguish the masters students, who formed in any case only a small part of my sample, where this is relevant to the understanding of the issues I am discussing.

3

Why they entered Postgraduate Study

One of the most important issues is whether there is any way of detecting, at the point at which they come into graduate study, which graduates are likely to be less successful at it. In particular, do their reasons for choosing to do graduate study show any common characteristic in their motivation, or lack of it, that marks them out as different from other students? This is one reason why I asked respondents, generally early in the interviews, to try to recall why they had entered postgraduate study. Another reason was that it was an essential part of the story of their experiences of graduate study, both for the individual case and for the group as a whole. Without this information some of the significance of what happened later would have been lost.

In asking this I stressed that I wanted to know what *at that time* had influenced their decision. When they had answered my question, I generally asked if anything else had influenced the decision, and continued asking until they had told me all they could remember of the background to their decision and why they had reached it. I also, where they did not tell me this spontaneously, asked at what stage they reached their decision, with whom they discussed it, whether they considered any alternatives, and so on. Each of these further questions stimulated the student's memory of his thoughts and feelings when he made the decision and the circumstances in which it was made.

All this gave me a complex interweaving of motives, influences, reasons and judgements that are difficult to summarize briefly. Although I shall be picking out some that seem to have been important, and looking at those separately, it has to be remembered that hardly any of the students mentioned only one reason for the decision to enter postgraduate study; many produced a substantial number. Moreover, each consideration will have interacted with others, sometimes in a simple way, but often in a rather complex manner. A common example of relatively simple relationships between various considerations is that, if a student was interested in a particular topic and wished to study it further, there can have been no obvious alternative sufficiently attractive to draw him away; also he will have made some assumptions about the pleasure of research and about his enjoyment of the scholarly life and the university world. The complexities are to be found in the other more individual reasons, in the nuances and in where the emphasis is placed.

THE ATTRACTION OF THE SUBJECT

Undoubtedly the most important influence on most students' decisions was the wish to study in greater depth a field in which they had a special interest. The following extracts give a little of the feeling of enjoyment of and enthusiasm for their topics that ran through many of the interviews.

> Well I wanted to do it because I really liked the subject. Geology really grabbed me.

> I'd always thoroughly enjoyed the work of Frances Hodgson Burnett. I'd read it. I'd been collecting it since I was about eleven.

> At that point probably I was interested in the subject primarily. (Research on an American poet)

> I felt that an undergraduate degree had opened up an awful lot of doors and I wanted to go through a few of them. Secondly, I got interested in Lamartine himself.

> It's the pleasure I got out of mathematics, I think. It's difficult to describe. Mathematics is rather like music, and although you don't necessarily compose and are not necessarily a musician you still get a lot of enjoyment out of music. I had no ambition to go on and use it in any sense.

> I didn't just want to do a PhD. I only wanted to do a PhD in this particular area of enquiry. (Industrial sociology)

> I was just fascinated with history. It was all I wanted to do at that stage, and they offered me a grant so I was keen to stay on.

> I think the main reason was that during the last year and a half I had spent as an undergraduate I became very interested in certain theoretical and empirical questions in economics, particularly concerned with the theory of income distribution. In particular I had been very much influenced by the ideas of one of the lecturers.

> As far as I can remember there were two things. One was that I was faced with the prospect of giving up so many years' work in languages, which didn't appeal to me. I felt that, having got so far, I would like to take it further. There was also the point that I had become quite interested in German baroque literature in the last year of my undergraduate course.

> I did really enjoy the subject. It was the subject that interested me. I wanted to continue doing that subject. (Mathematics)

THE ATTRACTION OF RESEARCH

The wish to study a subject in greater depth generally implied a wish to do research in it, but sometimes this was mentioned separately.

> Going into industry seemed to be more related to earning lots of money and so on, which I wasn't especially interested in; and doing research

seemed to me the sort of thing that would be more interesting of the alternatives. (Computing)

I then joined ...'s research group at .... I felt I wanted to do research. I did want to do research at the time; and he had a fairly large project which has recently got an award for the work that was done on it, and he was beyond what anyone else in the world was doing at the time, and it seemed more interesting, and I went into that. (Computing)

I was very attracted by the freedom and opportunity to research. The people who taught me for the most part were young, themselves researching actively, and a great deal of the time it was clear that what I was being taught came not from what they had read but from the development of their ideas by their research. (History)

Sometimes there was an especial stress on the attractiveness of the intellectual challenge offered by research.

I think it was really to test myself out. I still have the feeling that most things are interesting if you spend time getting into them and working them up. (Economics)

The concept of the project also fascinating me where one has a specific destination to reach even though it may not be defined and you have to perform the functions of planning the journey and supplying yourself and effecting the chain. (Electrical engineering)

I wanted to do a PhD and to do it in England particularly because I wanted to get away from taught courses. I wanted to do it entirely on my own devices because I didn't feel, from the time when I first started school, I had ever really been challenged by my studies. (Literature)

FOR A CAREER
Among those who entered postgraduate study for the sake of their eventual career, two groups need to be distinguished from the rest. First, those who had been following a wholly vocational course had, as one would expect, been doing so for vocational reasons – generally not so much to enter a field of employment as to further their careers within a field they had already entered. An example are students who had successfully completed diplomas in librarianship and were trying to add a masters to them.

Secondly, ten people were already embarked on a career in school teaching when they started their graduate studies, which most of them followed as part-time students, and they form a distinct group in a number of ways. One of them described her reasons for studying as 'Interest, just interest' and was quite sure that there had been no other element in her decision. Most of the others mentioned interest in a particular subject as having influenced them; but they mainly placed considerable emphasis on the value of the additional qualification to their careers. Perhaps it is in school teaching more than most occupations that paper qualifications are of value, helping to ensure that a candidate for a higher graded post will at least be short-listed for interview. An extreme example of this view was:

> Teaching has now got to the stage where you don't have to be a good teacher. You have to have a lot of qualifications in order to progress.

That I do not accept this as true is irrelevant; the teacher seemed to believe it. The same point was also put more moderately:

> I'd been on interviews and found that a 2.2 BEd wasn't really carrying much weight.

It is relevant that in two of these cases an important reason for the student having dropped out of graduate study was rapid promotion. Of course, the achievement of promotion without a higher degree was only part of the explanation for giving up, and the extra work resulting from promotion had some effect too.

The belief that a research degree would help a career outside the education system was mentioned from time to time. A chemist said that he believed the more senior posts in such firms as ICI were reserved for PhDs. A technologist described as 'peanuts' the salary of a civil service job she had been offered:

> So I thought to myself how can I improve my chances of getting an even better job. At that time it seemed to me the best thing was to get a higher degree – which later proved not to be valid.

A biologist said:

> I thought at the time that a career in research science was probably right for me. I thought it would make the best use of my abilities.

Other references to the usefulness of a higher degree outside the education system were mainly of a somewhat vague and rather general kind.

> I think it was just a fairly natural step to take, on the basis that a large number of people have a first degree, but overall to stand out a little bit more one should really have done something a little bit better. (Electrical engineering)

> I wasn't clear what sort of career I wanted to pursue; I was still thinking about that. I was thinking very much at that time of the Government Economic Service, but I thought again I wouldn't be doing myself any harm to stay on and do a further piece of postgraduate research.

Amongst those students who went straight from a first degree to graduate study, the wish to become a university teacher, or at least a teacher in some part of higher education, was found far more often.

> I think the first reason was much more wanting to teach in a university than research for research's sake. (Statistics)

> Well, I was interested in history and I was particularly interested in the idea of being a historian and it seemed a perfectly feasible thing to do, in job terms as it were, to press on.

I got a first in both my second and third year examinations and from mid-way through, I suppose about my second year, decided, for want of anything much better to do, that I would do a Phd. At that stage I thought I wanted to be a university teacher, but I certainly couldn't claim that I'd thought it out, that I'd considered the alternatives in any detail at all. (History)

I suppose I'd built up a picture of going to university, getting a degree, doing a PhD, and then getting a lectureship; so right from the start, really, of my first degree I'd had that in mind. (Mature student, biology)

I wanted to be a lecturer and I thought, 'Well, I have to get a PhD first'. I like teaching, but not in a school because too much of it is maintaining discipline rather than teaching. I thought of it purely as a necessary qualification to becoming a lecturer and I couldn't think of any other reason why anybody should want a PhD. (From his answers to further questions it emerged that another reason he wanted to become a lecturer was to do research, and he wanted to do research because of his dedication to mathematics.)

I think it was hope of an academic career. I think I was already thinking in those terms. Looking back, and particularly at the way things have become now, this was rather a quixotic and imprudent thing to *count* on doing. One might have *a hope* of doing it. I did find myself, after doing research for two or three years, in the position of feeling that, if I didn't get an academic job, my research would have been wasted, because to do research in medieval history, which I did, would not have been a sensible path to anything else really.
ER. Was there any other consideration in it?
I suppose I wasn't particularly attracted by anything else. In a sense it's an easy decision to make, to stay where you are already. (History lecturer in university)
In these answers there are links with the attraction of research, which has already been mentioned. There are stronger links, however, with the next reason I give for entry into graduate study.

DRIFT, INERTIA AND INDECISION

There were a number of ways in which entry into postgraduate study came not so much from a clear and firm decision as from drift, inertia and indecision. As the last extract put it, staying where you were already was the easiest decision to make. It was also a way of postponing a decision. Another is fear of the outside world, or at least a preference for the known world of the university. Students with firsts knew they could have a grant for the asking, and to do anything else was not so easy. Another is that students are the products of an education system within which the reward of success is to stay in the system longer. They had become conditioned to the idea that if they did well in their exams they would simply continue their education. They saw the PhD merely as the next rung of a ladder they were climbing (a number of students used the ladder simile). The decision to climb the ladder had been made long ago, and the alternative of getting off the ladder did not really occur to them. Their own expectation that they would continue climbing was reinforced by other people's expectation that that was what they would do.

This group of influences affected only those students who went directly from a first degree to graduate study.

> I think it was the result of having a first and not having anything particular to do afterwards. (Modern languages)

> Largely because I didn't have any clear idea of doing anything else. Having got a first I knew it was automatically available to me; and I think I felt really that it would probably be worth spending another three years at university and thinking about what I would want to do after. (English literature)

> ER. Looking back, can you remember why you wanted to do research?
> No; and I wasn't very sure at the time either. It was, I would say, at least half not being able to identify anything, any other organization, to work for. I expect quite important would be that a lot of people I knew were staying on. (Electrical engineering)

> There was one other point, which was I couldn't think what else I was going to do, which is a situation I still find myself in, so research was a way of keeping me interested in something while I made up my mind. (Modern languages)

> I suppose there was a certain lack of confidence in going out into the big wide world, and '72 wasn't a particularly good year for going out into the big wide world anyway. (Computing)

> ER. Had you thought of a career at that point (graduation)?
> No, I hadn't really. I think it was the security of having a first that made those questions more distant than they might have been. (Electrical engineering)

> It just happened really. It wasn't a conscious choice amongst alternatives. (Psychology)

> There was a sense of the unknown if you moved on from university life. (Botany)

> I think it really came about by default because I really didn't have very much idea of wanting to do anything, or any sort of work, I hadn't got much clue about the outside world at all. (Psychology)

> For a number of reasons. One was that it's easy to see that as being the next logical thing to do if you've been in an education system which pushes you up like rungs up a ladder and you do your O levels and then you do your A levels; and then you can apply for university, so you do; and then the next most logical thing to do is research, so that makes it an

easy decision to make - in some senses, easier than choosing to stop being on that particular ladder. (Modern language)

To some extent it was a natural progression. The path was all laid out in front. It's an extremely easy way to go. (Vet – research degree)

I'd been having quite a successful undergraduate career, so it was suggested to me by the lecturers there that I should think of going on to research, and they were reasonably confident that if I continued in the way I was going I should get a quota award. And so really I just took it for granted. It's a bit like when you are at school and you go on to university. It sort of gets built in. Expectations start being set for you by other people, and you just follow through with these expectations. (Anthropology)

THE ATTRACTIONS OF UNIVERSITY LIFE

Some graduates' reasons for entering postgraduate study, while somewhat similar to the foregoing, went beyond a preference for the known world of the university over the unknown world outside, and laid more emphasis on a positive wish to go on enjoying university life.

I was enjoying being at university, and it was a continuation of that way of life. (Mathematics)

Well, one would have to say that one did enjoy the ambience a lot, although you recognize that it will be a bit Van Winklish and faces would go; but certainly that was a strong influence. (History)

I think the honest answer is that I wanted another year at....(Social psychology)

One could put it rather crudely and say that I just didn't want to go out. I didn't want to leave Oxbridge, didn't want to leave that kind of life and that particular kind of ability to do rewarding things; and research seemed the best way to do that. (English)

I wanted to continue the student existence that I'd found was so appealing.
    ER. What sort of things had you been involved in that you found so interesting?
    Girls. (Chemistry)

Generally those students who said they were influenced by the attractiveness of university life said that it was not any particular activity that they wanted to continue – just university life as a whole. However, one did want to go on rowing, another to continue playing football, and another to continue in local political activities, both town and university, with at least one eye on the possibility of a political career.

RECRUITMENT BY STAFF

Students frequently said they had been recruited into postgraduate study by staff acting as talent scouts. For example, a graduate who was in employment had seen a paper about a new technique that she thought might be applicable to her work. She wrote to the author, who suggested she enrol as a part-time research student at his university. This sort of case is relatively unusual. More commonly, staff look out for bright and congenial under-graduates to whom they suggest the possibility and offer the opportunity of doing a research degree, or just convey the assumption that this is what any right-minded graduate does.

> One or two staff had said during the course of my last undergraduate year that some of the work I was doing showed a bent more towards research than towards producing undergraduate essays. (Modern languages)

> I must admit there was an element of not having anything else very obvious to do. B..., who was to become my supervisor, offered me a studentship at the end of my second year, and so, I suppose, to an extent, I simply took that as the easiest course of action. (Zoology)

> He was keen to get a group of graduate students working in that field and to build it up. (Economics)

> The atmosphere we found as undergraduates was conducive to making one believe that research was what it was all about. The way the whole of the syllabus was taught was a research-oriented sort of thing – we were always using journals and doing pretend research projects – and everybody that considered themselves to be a biologist wanted to do research. Most of us applied. A lot didn't get places. It was made clear by the powers-that-be in the department that it was the thing to do. I remember one girl particularly who went to be an accountant who knew exactly where she was going – she wanted lots of money, she got a very highly paid job – and one of our lecturers said 'Well, Jane, a charming girl, but just not a biologist'.

There were other ways in which research students were recruited. An economist answered an advertisement offering a research studentship tenable in a multi-disciplinary team. A chemist had gone to a department which had written to the head of the department in which she had graduated asking if he had anyone to do a specific piece of PhD research.

> So it literally was offered to me rather than going out looking for it.

More widely, the offer of a grant was a powerful inducement to stay in the university.

One student said that while some of those of his contemporaries who gained good degrees were being encouraged to stay on for research, others were being discouraged. Another said that he had been encouraged by the staff who taught him for his first degree to follow it by a taught masters, at another university. The staff of his second university, in their turn, encouraged him to register for a research degree, elsewhere.

OTHERS' EXAMPLES OR EXPECTATIONS
Some of the comments already quoted have touched on the influence of

other people's expectation that the student would enter graduate study. Some students mentioned this influence more explicitly. The example of their fellow students also had an effect; seeing earlier generations of graduates staying on for higher degrees made this seem the normal and natural thing to do.

> Well it did seem to be the thing to do in that people did it. (Art history)

Some students seemed to be affected by both the example ·and the expectations of others. They mentioned that they had parents or older brothers or sisters who were university teachers or held PhDs. Similarly, some were influenced by the decision of a boy-friend, girl-friend, wife or husband to enter postgraduate study.

On the other hand one student explained a gap of a year between graduation and beginning graduate study as resulting in part from the hostility towards research of his family and even more of his undergraduate friends — a reminder that there are many student sub-cultures, not all of which accept the values of the university.

OTHER CONSIDERATIONS
The following were some minor influences that were reported by only a few students each.

a   A reaction against an uncongenial or unsatisfactory job.

> Well it was actually a decision. It wasn't drift. I was a bit fed-up with working in a planning office *per se*. I found it restrictive. (Geography)

> (Of previous job) And to a certain degree it satisfied quite a lot of what I was looking for, but it didn't really satisfy anything at all intellectually. (Archaeology)

b   The belief that both doing research and gaining a higher degree give status.

> The allure of the letters after one's name, and the general status involved, writing papers, rubbing shoulders with authorities, things like that. (Electrical engineering)

> Somebody once said to me, paraphrasing Marlow, 'Is it not passing brave to have the doctorate'.(English)

c   For part-time students and other mature students, to be subject to an external discipline.

> I found myself spending more and more of my income on books and enjoying what can only be called intellectual pleasures more than anything else. I'm also an extremely idle person and unless I've got the spur of something in front of me, I tend to watch Match of

the Day or whatever it may be; and so I wanted, to a degree, to stimulate my intellectual progress. I love finding out and I wouldn't have done so with such intensity unless I had a degree in front of me to force me. (English)

d For those on non-vocational taught courses, to fill in some of the gaps left by their first degrees.

I felt having spread myself over three fairly broad subjects I needed a little more detailed teaching.

e The relatively easy availability of money for postgraduate study.

When I graduated from Oxbridge I actually did apply to a number of organizations, such as British Steel, Unilever and others for a job, very uncertain as to what sort of job I would want. I didn't actually get offered any jobs. I don't know if you remember, 1970 was a period when employment was pretty bad, and I did get offered money to do postgraduate work, but my interest in it was simply one of a number of possibilities for the next year, and this happened to be the one that produced something definite, so, to an extent, I fell into it. (Politics)

THE INTERRELATIONSHIP OF INFLUENCES

I have already said, above, that most students mentioned a substantial number of circumstances and considerations that influenced their decision to enter graduate study, and that these were often interrelated. Some impression of how the complete picture would fit together may be given by the next three extracts. These cover some of the simpler cases − more complex ones might be identifiable.

ER. At what point did you decide it was research you were going to do?

Well, I think I'd known ever since I made the decision to do music, which was rather late in my sixth form career in fact.

ER. You'd already planned that far ahead?

I don't know that it was planned. It was just that it seemed to be the sort of thing I would do. I knew I wasn't going to be a professional performer. I thought it possible that I might teach, but I was never especially enamoured at that idea, and I'd always enjoyed doing research work of a fairly small-scale nature, as you do at school, so it seemed likely that that was what I'd do; and anyway the money situation was a bit easier then, and there was a likelihood that one would get a grant for a reasonably decent degree.

ER. Did you, at any point in your undergraduate career, consider any alternative seriously?

I was slightly pressed by the then head of department to consider working for the New Grove's Dictionary, which was just beginning when I was in my third year. There was what was advertised as a secretarial post − but what would have ended up as a sort of general administrative research assistant post — going, and he felt I might at least consider whether I wanted to do that, but I didn't particularly want to work in an office, although I have always enjoyed administrative work, and, at one stage, way back, thought about going into the civil service. It didn't then seem to be something I wanted to do, so there was, no, never really any serious alternative, except, much further back, when I thought about the civil service or possibly law.

Well, towards the end of the course it became obvious to me that I stood a chance of a first, and everybody said 'Well of course you'll want to do research won't you?'

ER. Who was everybody? Staff or other students?

Both, I think. So I made inquiries because I felt I ought to do that and I suppose things snowballed really. I didn't have any burning ambition to do it. At least I didn't go to university at the age of 18 with any burning ambition to stay on longer; but I think one thing led to another and I found myself doing it. Quite the wrong reasons probably that led me to it.

ER. Did you seriously consider any alternative?

Well, I knew I was going to be a teacher in the end, and I decided that whether I went into teaching at 22 or 25 wouldn't really make any difference in the context of a lifetime of teaching, so I was quite prepared to do the research because it would be something that I would not have the opportunity ever again to do. It would be foolish to turn down that particular opening, it seemed.

ER. I think that you are saying that you didn't really see it as an alternative to what you were intending to do but simply as a stage that could be interposed on the way to it.

Yes, that's right. It was something which was self-contained. I didn't really see myself as going on to be a university lecturer.

ER. What did you hope to get out of it when you went into it?

That's a very difficult question. I really don't know. I suppose lurking at the back of my mind was the fact that it would be nice to have a PhD, quite honestly. Sort of cachet about it. I think I was also genuinely interested in the topic that I started off researching. I think I probably had a genuine interest in that and I welcomed the opportunity to do some reading in that particular area. (English literature)

I believed it would lead me to, not exactly prosperity, but some security, because then, in 1969, there wasn't the decline of the academic world which is particularly manifest now. I also thought it would add status — there was an ego aspect about it. I suspect that a major component was that, if you had done well as an undergraduate you went on to postgraduate work. It was seen as the culmination of a successful undergraduate career. Those who got firsts tended to go into research and were respected. It is true that some people with firsts went into other professions, into industry, etc., but they were not well reported, I suspect, because undergraduates got to hear about the researchers because they were still around. Therefore, even if you didn't get the best degree, and I didn't, if you got the accolade just the same it looked as good. It was good to have the status of being a postgraduate. You would say 'I'm doing a doctorate'. Also I think one's formative years, from 17 to 20, had been in that kind of setting and I wanted to continue within it. I thought this was the world, and it was very pleasing. It was such a change. I'd come from a hard industrial background in the North to smooth, decadent, prosperous Bath. It was marvellous. I didn't want to go back to the back-streets of Liverpool. And also there was a political attitude at the time that the one thing you don't ever want to do was to go into industry because capitalism is the downfall of mankind — all of the ideological claptrap that I believed or was influenced by at the age of 20 when I was making these decisions. (Zoology)

SUMMING UP
This research was designed as a series of case studies and not to produce precise statistics of the percentage doing this and the percentage doing that. Nevertheless, to count the numbers giving each of the various explanations for why they entered postgraduate studies as part of the description of the group whose later misadventures will be reported below, provided it is remembered that only substantial differences in percentages can be taken to have much meaning.

It needs to be remembered that the frequency with which any category is recorded is not wholly independent of the number of categories. The more categories the greater the number of influences per students that will be

	No. of times mentioned	% of reasons mentioned
Devotion to, interest in, enjoyment of subject	58	17.8
For a career in higher education	31	9.5
Wish to do research, independent exploration, etc.	26	8.0
General advancement of career	22	6.8
The attractions of university life	20	6.2
Staff as recruiting agents	19	5.8
Indecision, drift, reluctance to enter outside world	18	5.5
Degree itself or status	17	5.2
Lack of alternatives	11	3.4
Example of others	9	2.8
Availability of grant	9	2.8
Educational ladder effect	8	2.5
Others' expectations	7	2.2
To enter a specific career (outside higher education)	6	1.8
To follow a taught course	6	1.8
More time for a decision	5	1.5
Wish for intellectual stimulation	5	1.5
Easiest decision to make	4	1.2
Poor first degree	4	1.2
For application of external discipline	4	1.2
Adverse experience of employment	4	1.2
Others	32	9.8
Total	325	

Table 3.1
The frequency with which students mentioned certain influences on their decision to enter postgraduate study (Number of cases = 104).

recorded. On the other hand, the more that categories which could be taken together are subdivided, the smaller the number of cases in each.

One further preliminary point: those reasons for the decision that imply drift or reluctance to enter the outside world are inapplicable to those of my sample who had decided to leave the university and then later, sometimes much later, came back. They formed a third of the total.

Respondents mentioned an average (arithmetic mean) of 3.1 influences each (median = 3; Q1 = 2; Q3 = 4).

Some students had undertaken more than one form of postgraduate study – for example a taught course followed by research. In such cases, if the first was followed immediately by the second period of study and it made sense to regard them as continuous, the reasons counted are the reasons for entry to both. Otherwise they are the reasons for entry only to the studies in which their lack of progress brought them into my sample.

The results of a count of the frequency with which the various influences on their decision were reported by the students are shown in Table 3.1.

As one would expect, devotion to, interest in or enjoyment either of the general subject area or the precise topic of the research was mentioned more often than any other influence. What is more surprising is that nearly half the students did not mention it. Next, fairly close together, and mentioned by about a quarter to a third each, came the wish for a career in higher education and the wish to do research, independent investigation, 'to do one's own thing', etc. Indecision, drift, and reluctance to enter the outside world come rather further down the list. This answer was, however, given by more than a quarter of those respondents who had decided to enter graduate study immediately on graduation. When this group of answers is taken together with other related answers* – the lack of a viable alternative, the wish for more time for decision, and graduate study being the easiest decision to make – this becomes the second most important group of answers for the relevant students.

COMPARISON WITH EARLIER SURVEYS

There are two sets of figures with which these results can be compared, arising from interviews with current graduate students mainly in 1965 (Rudd 1975) and from a postal survey of past graduate students in 1966 (Rudd and Hatch 1968).

The 1965 current students were presented with a list of reasons for entry to graduate study, developed in a pilot survey, and asked to say if any of these, or some other reason, was their main reason for entry, and similarly asked for their subsidiary reasons. The past students were presented with the same list, plus some minor additions, and asked to say for each whether it was a strong influence, of some influence or of no influence on their decision.

Table 3.2 shows the result of these questions. The groupings adopted were derived from a correlation analysis of the results of the postal survey – any respondent giving one of the answers within a group was relatively likely to give the others. It will be seen that the rank order of frequency with which

---

* A straightforward addition of numbers would produce some double-counting – some respondents gave more than one reason of this kind.

the various responses were given is similar to that to be found in my recent interviews — any attempt at a closer comparison would be hazardous. However, this comparison does suggest that, in this respect, my sample was not atypical.

	Successful students		Students not successful by 1966	
	% of students	% of reasons mentioned	% of students	% of reasons mentioned
Academic				
Interest in specialized field	79.7	14.6	83.0	16.8
Enjoyment of research	81.2	14.8	75.8	15.3
Wish to be university teacher	42.5	7.8	35.5	7.2
Vocational				
Better promotion prospects and salary	63.3	11.6	50.1	10.1
To enter career (other than university)	34.9	6.4	24.2	4.9
Inertia (etc.)				
Normal for anyone with good degree	48.3	8.8	42.2	8.5
Lack of preferable alternative	32.2	5.9	31.9	6.4
Enjoyment of university life	66.9	12.2	44.8	13.1
Other				
Cover up poor first degree	16.2	3.0	17.0	3.4
Honour of doctorate	45.3	8.3	42.7	8.6
Instigation of employer	7.3	1.3	9.0	1.8
Alternative of national service	29.4	5.3	19.3	3.9
Number of students	1465		389	
Number of reasons mentioned	8016		1927	
Reasons per student	5.5		5.0	

Table 3.2

Reasons that were either a strong influence or some influence on the decision to enter postgraduate study of 1957 entrants attempting to gain a higher degree: all universities in Great Britain.

The postal survey of 1957 entrants to postgraduate study also enabled a comparison to be made between those who, by the time of the survey, in 1966, had gained the qualifications at which they were aiming and those who had not. This shows that the less successful students were more likely to have come into postgraduate study through interest in a specialized field and less likely to have come in for vocational reasons or because it is normal for anyone with a good degree to do this. However, these differences could be accounted for by differences in the balance of the subjects studied. In the successful students there was a lower proportion of arts and social studies students and a higher proportion of science and technology students than in the less successful group; and arts students are more likely than others to have been influenced by interest in a specialized field, while technology students are more affected that others by vocational considerations and science students are most likely to go into graduate study because that is normal for anyone with a good degree.

Therefore it seems that there was no real and substantial difference in the reasons why they came into graduate study between the successful and the less successful entering in 1957. Taken together with the resemblance between the reasons for entry given in my recent interviews and those given in the past, it suggests that there is nothing conspicuous in this facet of students' motivation that would enable the less successful to be distinguished from the successful on entry simply by questions about their motivation.

This does not mean, however, that these reasons for entry are irrelevant to later success or failure. The circumstances that led to dropping out are rarely simple, and what brought the student in has some part in the story of what takes him out.

4

The Complexity of Causation

THE VARIOUS STAGES OF DELAY AND FAILURE

At undergraduate level a point is eventually reached at which a student has gained his degree, failed or given up. At postgraduate level, the categories of success or failure are more diverse and less clear-cut; and those into which my sample fell are shown in Table 4.1.

Given up studies	56
Failed totally	3
Awarded lesser degree	4
Submitted thesis – no result yet	3
Deferred – to re-submit	2
Draft with supervisor	4
Still studying – has been full-time student	17
Still studying – entirely part-time	3
Writing up (or written up) for publication but not for higher degree	4
Degree awarded	3
Not really started	3
Transferred between universities	2
Unclear	3
	106

Table 4.1
The sample: whether still attempting to obtain higher degree.

Only seven students in my sample had failed to gain the degrees they were attempting, and of these, four had been awarded a lesser degree – for example they might have submitted a PhD thesis for which they were awarded an MPhil.

Just over half (56) had given up their studies. Everyone for whom it was clear that completing was no more than an occasional pipe-dream was included here, together with those who said they had given up altogether and had no thought of resuming. In a further three cases (categorized as 'unclear'), although it was not clear that they had really given up, neither was it clear that they were genuinely continuing.

There were also three students who had barely started their studies for a higher degree at the universities that gave me their names. One had applied for two courses in the same field, but, as there was some uncertainty about whether his preferred course would be run, he went to his second-choice university, leaving after a few days on hearing that the other course was available. He gained the masters at which he was aiming. A second of this group was interviewed only over the telephone and so does not appear elsewhere in my account. He went to a university and started a course, but after a few days, and before he had paid any fees, decided he really wanted to do a quite different course in a different subject on the other side of the Atlantic, and so left. The third was a research assistant who applied to register for a PhD, but found there was no way he could avoid paying the full fees, which rose sharply that year, and he decided that a PhD was not worth all that money.

Two other students could not really be included either in the drop-outs or those who were taking an excessive time. They came into my list because they had left a university without completing the degrees for which they had registered; but they had done this in order to complete their studies elsewhere. One had initially accepted a research assistantship which enabled him to register for a PhD, but found himself working under a jet-set professor and allowed very little time for PhD work. He was therefore likely to gain neither an adequate training in research nor a higher degree. At the end of the first year he left to become a research student elsewhere.

The other was a mature student with a weak first degree, who went to do a PhD at the only university that would accept him. He was in a small department, and although receiving helpful and conscientious supervision, felt the lack of opportunities to interact with others having similar interests. A chance meeting produced the opportunity for him to move to a large department in a prestigious university, which, moreover, was nearer his home, and he took it.

By the time I interviewed them, which was sometimes a year or more after I first contacted them, a further six students had completed their studies, at least for the present, three having been awarded PhDs and three having submitted theses but not yet heard the result. Their experiences were still relevant to my study as they had all taken a long time completing their theses.

The remaining thirty were still continuing their studies with varying degrees of assiduity. Some had completed draft theses and were awaiting their supervisors' comments. Some said they were very close to completion; and one, having submitted a thesis that had been referred, said that he was not far from finishing the rewriting of it for resubmission.

At the other extreme were some who were continuing their research in what seemed to me to be an obsessive rather than a purposeful manner and of whom it seemed reasonable to doubt if they would ever complete.

Amongst those still working on their theses, two groups need to be separately distinguished. First, when my sample was being identified, the criteria used in certain universities for distinguishing those students who had been dilatory in their studies resulted in my being put in touch with some part-time students who, although they could hardly be accused of having been over-hasty in their studies, had not, nevertheless, for part-time students, spent a markedly excessive time.

Secondly, four students had decided that the results of their research were more suited to presentation in the form of published articles, or a book, than to a thesis, and had written and were continuing to write for immediate publication.

CAUSATION

Road accidents rarely have a single cause: often, if any one of a whole collection of circumstances were absent, the accident would not have happened — if, for example, the car had had more tread on its tyres, the road surface had offered more skidding resistance, it had not been wet, visibility had been better, the car was not being driven at a speed at which it could not stop within the limits of the driver's visibility, and the pedestrian, cyclist, other car, or whatever, had not been on the road.

Similarly, there is rarely a single cause for a graduate student's failure to achieve a higher degree; and often the absence of any one or two in a whole series of interconnected causes could have meant the student would have completed his studies in a reasonable time. Usually the causes are connected with research in that he or she either was a research student or successfully followed a taught course but failed to complete the dissertation necessary for the masters degree. Commonly the student, although gifted in other ways, showed no flair for research, had failed to plan his work properly, or to follow any plans for timing that he had made, and was neither very energetic nor very strongly motivated towards the research. Nevertheless, the failure might have been avoided if the process of initial selection had included any adequate test of the student's suitability, or if the supervisor had given adequate and sufficiently clear guidance and applied sufficient pressure. Even without this the student might have finished eventually if some final precipitating event had not brought him to a halt — a change in his job that left him less spare time, the break-up of a marriage, an illness, injury or baby, or even, in one bizarre case, the loss of the partly written thesis, notes, etc. when moving house.

To make the discussion intelligible, I have to take each cause of slow progress or failure separately, leaving it to the reader to remember, however, that they rarely occur in isolation.

I have divided the factors contributing to failure or slowness into five groups:

a The qualities of the student.
b Personal and individual problems and accidents not directly arising from the student's studies.
c Problems inherent in the research.
d Personal academic problems other than teaching and supervision.
e Teaching and supervision.

As with most classification systems, there is a tendency for these groups to merge and overlap a little at the edges.

5

The Qualities of the Student

THE STUDENT'S ABILITIES

The most obvious area in which to look for qualities that predestine a student to failure is in his aptitude for the studies he is attempting. Yet in only two cases did my interviews give me a strong feeling that the person I was interviewing did not have the ability to follow postgraduate study of some kind. I am not saying that all the others had the ability; only that any such lack of ability was not apparent to me in the course of fairly searching interviews. Moreover, in both cases where there did seem to be lack of ability, there were other, contributory factors. Both were mature students who had left the standard educational ladder early and made their way up by other routes. Therefore, if I myself had been interviewing them for a postgraduate place, I would have been strongly tempted, from considerations of equity, to give them a chance. Also both had suffered an illness or an accident, but had chosen, perhaps mistakenly, not to withdraw in order to repeat the year — both were following taught courses.

I am certainly not saying here that lack of ability played no part in these failures. I would draw a quite different conclusion — that it is very difficult, at postgraduate level, to discover from a student's scholastic record and an interview whether he has the requisite ability for postgraduate study. Any attempt to increase completion rates by better selection will need to be substantially more sophisticated than this — a point to which I will return below.

There were also a few cases where, in the student's view, he did not have the relevant abilities for the kind of postgraduate work he was doing. One PhD student discovered that his forte lay in developing experimental methods and techniques that would be of use to others rather than in following a piece of research through all its stages. Two other students found that, whereas they were good at achieving practical results — a piece of hardware, a computer programme that worked — they were unable to make the jump from their results to theory. All three had brilliant first degrees, and in a way, all three had been very successful, at least in their subsequent careers. They had gained much, and especially knowledge of where their abilities lay, from their periods as research students. But their gains did not include a PhD, and if they were right in their judgement of their own capabilities, they probably did not have the ability to gain one. I doubt whether there is any way in which this lack could be detected until a fairly late stage of the research.

There is one ability or skill that is universally necessary for the achievement – in good time – of a higher degree – the ability to write reasonably rapidly. The lack of this seemed to be the main cause of delay for some of the students, especially those who were still working for PhDs. It ought to be easier to detect at an early stage. The problem is how far the ability to write quickly is an inherent ability, and how far it is a skill which, even at this late stage of a student's education, can still be imparted.

There is a further problem here. If a student told me that he wrote rather slowly, or if the time he had spent on each chapter of his thesis showed that he was writing very slowly, it would not necessarily mean that all his writing was always slow. In the arts and social studies it would be difficult for anyone who, for example, was always slow in composing sentences, to advance far within an educational system where success is measured by performance in examinations which demand the ability to write short essays in answer to previously unseen questions within a brief set period.

Surely, for most people writing non-fiction (other than journalists), speed of writing is related to understanding of the subject and clarity of thought. The students' slowness in writing may mean that they do not know what they want to say rather than that they have difficulty putting their ideas into words and stringing together what they want to say into sentences, paragraphs and chapters. Slowness in writing-up could be just another symptom of a general slowness at, and ineptitude for research.

PREVIOUS STUDIES AND EXPERIENCE

In a number of cases students told me that they had been badly delayed by some substantial lack in the knowledge and skills they had brought from their earlier studies. In other cases, where I myself have some expertise in fields not too far from those of the students, I formed the view that the students' earlier studies, background and experience were very far from adequate for the course of study or research they were attempting. My impression that Education departments are especially ready to accept ill-prepared students may have sprung partly, but only partly, from my own special knowledge of the kinds of competence needed for research in Education.

Most of these cases came into three groups:

a Where a small amount of help and instruction from another department – perhaps in some aspect of computing, or the application of a highly specialized field of mathematics to an engineering problem – would have sufficed.

b Where the student needed a substantial course of instruction in specialized research techniques.

c Where the research required skills or techniques which it was beyond the student's power to master; for example, a student doing research in engineering said that he had not realized when he started that his topic would have a substantial mathematical content. At undergraduate level he had gone as far in mathematics as he was capable of going, and the work he now needed to do was beyond his abilities. Some of the students I met who had this kind of difficulty should not have been doing research at all; others should have taken a different topic, or found some way of changing direction.

d Where the student was a very substantial distance from having followed studies at an appropriate level to permit him to undertake the form of postgraduate study for which he was accepted. One example was a mature student and a maverick. I would have guessed that the student had the ability to undertake some form of postgraduate study, possibly leading eventually to research, but was very far from having an adequate background of first degree level studies to be able to proceed immediately to part-time and very independent research carried out at some distance from the university. The student was aware of this and said:

> It bothers me now, in retrospect, that I would go into (large provincial) university and I would get onto a course of research – I could have my topic discussed by the faculty and approved – and knowing full well that my background really wasn't up to it. That bothers me.

The major issues examplified by these cases – co-operation between departments, preliminary instruction in research, the selection of students and the choice of topic for a PhD thesis or a masters dissertation will crop up again in wider contexts, and will be dealt with below. There is, however, one other, very specific, problem in this area that does not come into any such categories.

The problem concerns research in statistical theory, and arises from a difference between statistics and other subjects in that statistics has a more precarious existence as a 'pure' subject detached from its application. A masters degree student in statistics (not in my sample) told me that she would not take the PhD place available to her unless she were unable to find a satisfying job, as she felt she needed practical experience in the subject before she would be ready to advance its theory. Nor would she know what applied problems were important at that stage. A student in my sample said: 'The understanding of theoretical statistics comes from real statistics in a way, and until you understand the applications of what you're doing you can never really understand why you're doing it. I think that was one of the big problems I found.' And again: 'I never really had the grasp for the subject to actually be able to get anywhere with it. I understood the work that had been done but I didn't understand it well enough to see what you could do next.'

It seems to me that there is a strong case for British research students in statistics no longer being recruited from new graduates or students who have just completed a postgraduate taught course. Instead, more use should be made of the various schemes by which graduates in employment can, under the guidance of a university department, use work done for their employer for a PhD.

BOREDOM, DISENCHANTMENT, LAZINESS AND THE WORK ETHIC
Two masters degree students who frankly admitted that they had not done much academic work had gone into postgraduate study to be able to put time into political activities. One said he was surprised that he had been able to get

away with it, which raises issues to be discussed under the general heading of supervision.

Seven students gave up their research largely because they were not enjoying it — four of them during their first year. One of them summed up well what all four said: 'I realized that I had been romanticizing research somewhat, and there is a large element of routine in research work.'

One of the seven was a very complex case where a large number of factors interacted. All the other six had one feature in common — that they were working on topics that had been set for them or suggested to them by others; indeed three had taken research posts that had been advertised. In each case, the feeling building up that they did not really like research included an element of not liking the particular topic — 'It was much more laboratories and greenhouses rather than greenhouses and field plants.'

One of these six seems at first sight an especially strange case. He had, to his great surprise, in his final undergraduate year, been invited by a member of staff for whom he had a great respect to apply for a place as a research student, and had been allocated one of the department's research council awards. He decided to take a year off before beginning the research and took a job that he was much enjoying. The thought of giving it up and going back to the university made him miserable, but, nevertheless, he went back. He was casting about for a research topic and took one that had been suggested to him, but quickly realized that he did not have the necessary background knowledge and skills to do it effectively. He then continued for three years reading or pretending to read and doing little else — 'I used to sit and read books for hours and not know what I'd read at the end of it.'

Sitting staring at the page without taking in what it says is unsurprisingly common. One student said:

> It was a feeling that you had it there somewhere, but just couldn't get it quite to click; so you'd spend days and days — just sat staring blankly at the page — and eventually it would click.

Some of those for whom it never did click, and who gradually did less and less without making a clean break and giving up, seemed to accept this kind of idleness, due to their inability to cope, with a kind of relief. The tendency to go through the motions of research without doing it instead of firmly and definitely giving up, or even to plod on more actively well beyond the point where it is clear there is no hope of success, is probably due in part to the high status research holds in the universities. Once a student has been offered an opportunity to do research, it is an admission of more than just failure, an admission of the lack of some basic quality, rather like a lack of virility, to give up.

> I think someone would have done me a favour if they'd told me to go at the end of the first year. It would have hurt my pride, but I would have wasted a lot less time, and less of the research council's money.

Wrapped up with this is the problem that the student who is easily influenced into entering research is just not a very decisive sort of person.

I don't think I'm what you might call self-directed, in that I didn't feel my life was in my own hands. Somehow the wheels seemed to turn and... I'm going to mix my metaphors!

ER. You got carried along with the current, to produce another metaphor for you.

Yes. Really I was a bit of a mess, I think.

In addition to those students for whom boredom or disenchantment with research was the main reason for giving up their research, there were others for whom it may have been a contributory factor; if boredom results in a student not working sufficiently hard, a whole series of other things go wrong which may, in the end, produce a lack of results, or other reasons for failing or giving up the attempt to complete the work after the end of the normal three years.

Some students who said they had not been working as hard as they felt they should have done attributed this to boredom with the detailed work of research.

One thing I did learn about this sort of ecological research is that it's, well not even ninety per cent, it's about ninety-eight per cent just routine drudgery, which I've never been that good at, I must admit. Perhaps if I'd been better at knuckling down to some drudgery I might have got on a bit faster. But I never felt, you know, sort of 'Eureka! I've discovered something great here'. Another thing I feel about a lot of research — certainly postgrad research from my own experience and seeing those around me — is that a lot of it is really pretty trivial and pretty dull stuff to do.

A student who did in fact gain a PhD described this kind of boredom:

One starts early on to question why you're there, because the bandwaggon effect of undergraduate work disappears about a year after you've got into the PhD, because you're no longer involved in that corporate body, you don't have to attend lectures, you don't have official things you must do, you don't have to attend a specific tutorial. In other words there are no longer any clear stepping stones. The only stepping stone is to submit a thesis, and you ask 'Why?'. I think most people are disillusioned after about eighteen months. I think that's a normal phenomenon; you know — 'I'm pissed off with the whole thing. I'm not going to do it', etc. — and they come through it. But I noticed it very clearly then in many people, and it's a growing number. I don't know why. And the basis of it is 'Is it contributing anything to science or the arts or whatever? Is it contributing to me? Career? Status?' I certainly don't think it has anything in the way of status any more. Oh, you put Doctor in front of your name and that's a little bit of an ego trip, certainly; but a PhD doesn't mean anything to lay people.

This brings us to the question of motivation, which I shall discuss below. Before coming to that issue, however, I should, perhaps, put these cases in perspective. The students who had not, apparently, been working hard, for whatever reason, seemed a small minority of those I saw. For most, these had been years of unremitting toil. Indeed, some may have worked too hard and might have been more successful if they had eased up a little.

> I think I did suffer a bit from a kind of puritan work ethic and didn't allow myself to relax. I mean, I never had a vacation until this summer — the first holiday I've had and relaxed since I started work on the thesis. What I'm sure I should have done now is gone on a holiday for a couple of weeks or a month.

MOTIVATION

There is a risk of a tautology in discussing motivation. One knows that to gain a higher degree requires effort. It is easy, therefore, both for the student trying to explain his lack of success and for the commentator to assume that lack of success implies too little effort; and too little effort implies that the student did not sufficiently strongly wish to succeed, or, in the current jargon, lacked motivation. So a lack of motivation is defined in a way that equates it with failure. This is a possibility that has to be kept in mind in considering the many references to a lack of motivation that students made.

Also we must remember the fox and the grapes. When one has failed to do something it is very tempting to say 'I didn't really want to do it, anyway.'

Having entered this caveat, I will now look at those cases where respondents either made some reference to motivation themselves or made it clear that, in deciding the order in which they ranked the potential uses of their time, they gave a higher ranking to other alternatives than to completing their theses. Such references were fairly frequent: for example, 'I could certainly, if I had been more single-minded, have got it finished before the problems of ... effectively drew a deadline before I was expecting to meet that deadline.' Or again: 'I think probably because I wasn't sufficiently keen to do it. If I am honest I think that was it.'

Several students spoke of the way in which, after contact with a supervisor, or other members of the department, or, in one case, a parent who, while in a rather different field, knew enough to discuss the student's work with him, they became fired with enthusiasm, for a while, but this gradually petered out, until it was renewed at the next similar contact. One said: 'Whenever I talk about it to anybody I get enthusiastic again.' Another said: 'I do need a push, and I haven't got that here.' Another, again, said: 'Although I know self-motivation is supposed to be the great thing, you do need a bit of encouragement from other people.' They themselves did not have a strong enough urge to do the work; it had to come from outside.

Another student spelt out more fully the same point: 'I think the truth of the matter is that I didn't have the external combination of support and pressure to make me really do what I could in terms of a PhD. That didn't exist, and I just didn't have the inner direction to provide it myself.'

However, most students did not blame others for their own lack of drive. A more typical comment was: 'I have been saying things about my supervisor, saying he was a lousy supervisor. I think, to be fair I should also say I was a lousy PhD student in that I didn't have enough motivation to go on.' And there was this comment from a wife who joined in the interview with her husband. She had started her PhD at the same time as he had, and had completed hers (there was more than one such case). She said 'I think I am a bit more tenacious perhaps.'

A number of students, especially masters students, said that the degree itself was not worth the effort they would have to put into finishing it off.

> I didn't give a damn about getting the qualification because, apart of course from the personal satisfaction one gets from completing the thing, it wasn't important, whereas, up to that point, O levels had seemed important and A levels seemed important if one wanted to go to university, which was important for getting a job.

> It was certainly no consequence to me whether I got a PhD – absolutely none at all – because I had no idea what I would do with it.

> And another reason I think is I'm not sure how useful completing is going to be to me in the sort of career I see myself pursuing.
> ER. What sort of career do you see yourself pursuing?
> Well, I don't think I would be inclined to go for teaching and that sort of academic career.
> ER. You mean university teaching?
> That's right. Yes. I may continue doing research either for university or civil service or something like that.

In all these comments there was the recurring theme that a higher degree was no use in a career, or at least in the kinds of career they expected to have – and who is to say they were wrong?

Another group of comments related to the things the students had to do that they claimed prevented them from getting on with the writing.

> At that stage I was trying to write up; but I was also renovating a house, laying concrete floors, and bathrooms, and putting in ceilings and wiring and all that sort of thing as well. So my writing-up became more and more the last thing I did on any one day.

> I have a family, a wife, a baby of two and people don't pay to write theses on Mahler. I'm very happy to be in this job partly because I enjoy the varied aspect of it, partly because it pays a living salary, which is important. But I feel I do need some kind of breathing space because it is fairly demanding – it is more than a nine to five job. And so, if I were to say, 'Could I spend evenings and week-ends at it?' 'With difficulty', I would say, because then I just simply wouldn't see the light of day.

Both of these students (and others) were saying that, at the margin of choice, when deciding whether to do a little more of this and a little less of that, other things took precedence over the thesis. (To put their arguments a little more into perspective, I should add that I do know, from personal experience that it is possible to spend one's spare time writing a thesis while in a demanding job and with a young family, with more serious problems than those students mentioned and with various other commitments. However, I cannot honestly recommend it.) I am sure that in many cases if

the students had sufficiently wanted to gain their higher degrees they would
have done it.

This issue of choice between activities was put more clearly by three other
students.

> I was very interested in music. I was in a choir at one stage. During the
> winter I would prefer to go out in the evening and meet people in the
> local pub rather than do anything connected with my research project.

> Getting down to it is what's stopping me, basically, because I find a lot of
> other things that I enjoy doing that are more pressing, for one reason or
> another.

> I took about three months off between the September of coming up here
> and Christmas — I didn't start work until the January. I really had been
> intending during that period to try to write the thing up; but I suppose I
> tended to use the new house and getting all the things there sorted out as
> a bit of an excuse. But really the enthusiasm had gone and I didn't feel
> that, for the effort involved, I had something substantial enough to get. I
> wouldn't really be communicating enough to people in general to be
> worth the bother.

Other students said they did not think the degree was worth the extra fees
they would have to pay to register as continuation students after their grants
had run out.

An unusual explanation for a lack of motivation was:

> Having got a double first you put that on a form, and not having a PhD
> doesn't matter because people are sufficiently impressed by that. Now I
> feel that has been a positive drawback because I feel perhaps if I'd have
> only got a 2.1 I'd have perhaps worked a bit harder to get a PhD in order
> to see myself as sufficiently qualified for some of the things that I've gone
> for.

An informant who has become a university teacher summed up especially
well:

> I have sometimes wondered how I would order the principal reasons for
> my failure to obtain a higher degree by research when I was registered in
> one way or another for a higher degree by research for six years, and the
> obvious conclusion I reach is that there were no insuperable obstacles had
> I had sufficient energy and will to carry out the research. People have
> produced research under just as difficult circumstances and it is that
> persistent enthusiasm which distinguishes those of us who get these
> qualifications and those of us that don't. I don't think the obstacles that I
> encountered were unusual. They varied; they covered a different pattern
> to other people, but they had the same sort of ingredients.

Perhaps I should add that this student's problems were indeed as severe as
those of most of the students I saw.

A last comment on motivation sums up my own view:

I have a feeling that it would be very much better if the people who did research were the people who ran round in small circles saying 'I want to work on this', even if they changed their minds and worked on something else — the people who really push at slightly closed doors and say 'I want to work on this; I want to work on this'.

6

Personal and Individual Problems other than Study Problems

INJURY OR ILLNESS

It is in cases of injury or illness that, if anywhere, one would expect to find a simple, uncomplicated explanation for a student withdrawing from post-graduate study, or failing to complete it within a reasonable time. I may be biased as, while writing this, I have been only too painfully aware of the way in which injury or illness, and the drugs prescribed for them, can slow one's writing and impair the will to continue. Nevertheless, none of the seven cases where the student reported some injury or illness was wholly straightfor-ward; in each of them there were other factors.

The simplest case was that of a student who was six months off finishing his thesis when he was hit by a car that left the road and crashed into a building. His skull was fractured and he spent six months in hospital – 'three months of which I was unconscious, and you can't write up when you are unconscious.' After this came a period of convalescence, when he had to be watched by a nurse all the time. Clearly he had every reason to do no work on his thesis for about a year and then to spend a period of some months working his way back into his research, remembering what his notes meant, what he had been about to do next and what he had intended to write.

It is at this stage that the complications appear, for his thesis was submitted, not some two years after the accident, but six years later. There was a complex and interrelated series of reasons for this, but chief among them was the fact that other things had not been standing still while he had been out of action. Before the accident he had been offered and had accepted a job which he was to take up six months later; so when he was sufficiently recovered he had to go and start work. In any case, his income as a student had by then stopped.

Usually, anyone who starts a job when his thesis is not yet completed finds that, initially, his new job leaves him little spare time and energy. It is not until he has learnt the job and settled, to some extent, into a routine, that the work on the thesis can be resumed. This student, however, did not resume the thesis. His explanations are too individual to be relevant here, or even to be repeated without breach of anonymity, but his comment on them is not:

I'm making excuses. I probably could have done some, but I didn't.

It seemed to me that in this student's comments — and in those I heard from many other students — there was a certain amount of the protestant work ethic making the student feel guilty that he had not been writing his thesis under difficult circumstances, and perhaps we are getting another aspect of the same thing in a comment he made about the period after he had returned to the university at which he had done his research when he was supporting himself as best he could while he resumed his PhD:

> When you return you have to rethink yourself into that kind of self-motivation.

However, the protestant work ethic is, after all, a kind of motivation and plainly his motivation was not, while he was in employment, strong enough for him to overcome the difficulties.

A quite different kind of case was a student whose broken ankle prevented him from taking part in a physical activity in which he had been taking a great delight — an activity which has both aesthetic and intellectual appeal (especially for people attracted by computing) and produces the same kind of addiction as bridge. This had so bad an effect on his morale that he virtually gave up his research.

He discussed with me his very different reaction to earlier breaking his wrist — it was in plaster when he took his examinations at the end of his second undergraduate year:

> Can you imagine doing a practical exam with your arm in a pot? Well I did anyway and I think I was induced to work so hard at revising that I in fact got a first. It was terribly hard work to do the same again the next year. So I think there the accident acted as a stimulus and tricked me into working harder than I would have.

His explanation was that breaking his ankle kept him away from an activity that was essential to his morale, but breaking anything else would not affect his morale in the same way. It was clear, however, that this was a gross over-simplification, and that a lot of other things were going wrong with his research. If he had been really dedicated to his research topic (and he was not), if his research had been going well (whereas it was in a cul de sac), if he had not discovered that his talents really lay in quite a different direction, he would have weathered a temporary absence from his favourite activity, using his enjoyment of his research to maintain his morale. As it was, the broken ankle merely provided the event that brought effective work to an end — which would have happened anyway — and perhaps a support to his *amour propre* when he might otherwise have felt a greater sense of failure.

So, even where the obstacle to completing postgraduate study was an injury or physical illness, there was often some lack of motivation involved as well.

The issues surrounding mental sickness — for a research student one of the most disabling illnesses — are even more complex. One student was quite clearly schizophrenic. Some mentioned depressive and other mental illness, and other similar personality problems — one said her work had been affected by the need to come to terms with her homosexuality.

Again, however, these are circumstances in which the chain of causation is not wholly clear. Did the strain of postgraduate study bring on or accentuate the mental illness? Did the illness alone bring about the failure? Or was there a more complex interaction, with the problems and difficulties of postgraduate study aggravating the problem of mental health, which in its turn made study more difficult, producing a downward spiral?

All these cases must have set difficult, painful, problems for the supervisors, and I would not wish to have been in their shoes. However, I suspect that in some of these cases the student should not have come into graduate study at all; and so the search for better ways of selecting students, and, even more important, for better ways of enabling students to make an informed choice of whether to enter postgraduate study, to which I shall turn in Chapter 11, is relevant in these cases too.

MARRIAGE AND MARITAL BREAKDOWN

I did not ask the people I interviewed about their marriages, but nine of them spontaneously mentioned to me that they had had a divorce. This is therefore a minimum number; there may have been others.

I have attempted to compare this number with the number that could have been expected if the divorce rates of all males and females (separately) aged 20-29 in England and Wales had applied to my respondents over the five-year period 1972-76. There are a number of simplifying assumptions in such a calculation. One is that my respondents could be expected to follow the standard pattern of marriage of their contemporaries in that period; but we know that graduates marry later than non-graduates (Kelsall, Poole and Kuhn 1972) and so we could expect fewer divorces in our group. The tendency for divorce to be disproportionately common in the working class would have a similar effect on the comparison.

Ignoring, unavoidably, all these points, I found that the proportion who were divorced in my group was almost twice as high as could be expected, the disparity being greatest amongst the women. On numbers of this kind, and given the assumptions involved, this difference should not be treated as if it were statistically significant. However, I suspect that a difference of this kind would be found if a larger group could be studied more carefully (in this respect) and so I think it worth considering possible explanations.

There are three, which are not mutually exclusive, that are especially obvious. The first is that working for a higher degree places a substantial strain on a marriage. The student's income is much lower than it would be if he were in a job, while at the same time he has less time to spare for his spouse, less time to do the various domestic chores and to spend on the children. This may especially affect the women students as women are traditionally expected to put more into the maintenance of a shared home and of a family than men. One woman, in comparing herself with the male students around her said:

I always had on my mind what I was going to have for dinner tonight, perhaps if I should be ironing my husband's socks, whereas they were much more single-minded in their approach to the work.

We must, regretfully, leave on one side the fascinating question of why a woman science graduate should, in the last quarter of the twentieth century, believe it necessary to iron socks, and merely take it that she was saying she had more domestic chores.

On the other hand, a number of respondents said how supportive their spouses had been, and how determined that they should succeed. Indeed, the husband of the student I have just quoted played an important part in persuading and helping her to resume work on her PhD so that she did, belatedly, gain the degree.

The second possible explanation looks at the effect of divorce on a postgraduate student. Both marital breakdown and divorce produce mental and emotional strains that make it more difficult for a student to concentrate and work steadily. Even after a period of recovery, it is difficult to pick up the threads and resume. Also the time that has been lost is gone for ever. Moreover, the spouse may have been contributing heavily to the student's financial support, and lack of money may force him or her to give up.

The third possible explanation for a high rate of marriage failure amongst my sample is that some of the qualities needed for success in postgraduate study are also qualities that are needed for success in marriage: for example, an aptitude for personal relationships, the ability to hear and take in what other people are saying, the ability to see the solution to a problem quickly, discrimination (in the choice of a problem and of a partner), a determination to succeed and a willingness to make sacrifices in the cause of success.

However, this cannot be more than speculation. To know whether there is a stronger link between failure in postgraduate studies and marital failure than between any postgraduate study, successful or not, and marital failure, we would need substantially more information than is available to us.

In most cases, marriage helps the student through his or her studies, providing every kind of support and encouragement, as well as companionship and stability. In only a few cases, where the spouse is unsympathetic to the whole idea of further studies, or grudges the sacrifices that both have to make, does the marriage itself become an impediment. In general, what interferes with postgraduate study is not marriage but a family. It is here, and only here, that there is a sharp divide between the experience of the men and the women I interviewed.

Many of the special difficulties the women meet are clear and obvious. On one occasion they were dramatically illustrated by the need to cut short an interview when my informant was phoned by her child's school and asked to collect him as he had been taken ill. However, in the half dozen or so cases where it emerged during the interview that my respondent's spouse had succeeded in gaining a higher degree, rather more than half of the successful spouses were women, which at least suggests that I ought to be somewhat cautious in suggesting that married women are overall under an especial handicap as graduate students. It is at least possible that some women are under no disadvantage, and that, for some of the others, there may be advantages that balance the disadvantages.

The difficulties for the woman generally start with the effect on her research of the nausea and other medical problems of pregnancy. Then, for most women, there is likely to be a period of some years between the birth of the first child and when the youngest starts school during which they are unlikely to be free from distractions for sufficiently long at a stretch to enable them to make real progress with the research or writing.

Some manage to find time if they are lucky in their child-minding arrangements. Others may be able to organize their day so that they have some free time. One of my sample had managed to complete her thesis when her children were still at home because the flexibility of her (self-employed) husband's working hours made it possible for him to look after the children while she went to the university, and she had uninterrupted evenings when the children were in bed. In another case, where I was interviewing a man whose wife had also been a student but had been more successful than him, the wife spoke of the way in which sharing child-rearing had made it possible for her to complete her PhD. But few men have the freedom to vary their working hours. Also here, as elsewhere, it was largely the problems of the unsuccessful that I was looking at, and I did not generally hear how the more successful had overcome them.

Here are some typical examples of the obstacles entailed in bringing up a family:

> Then I got pregnant and became very, very tired and left work and Mary was born, and there I was, stuck in this village with no means of getting in to the university, and somehow it just lapsed, and I thought, well, this is temporary, it'll just lie fallow for a bit, but like so many things... I think in some ways the impetus had gone out of it, and one is so totally taken up with a new baby that you just don't think of it, even though you think I must do this, that and the other. I did lots of things, but this was something which I hadn't really got enough time at a stretch to make it worth going into the university and doing some work. The odd hour just wasn't enough. You need the whole morning or a whole day really to get stuck into it. And also you've got to be able to do it often enough to keep your hand in, remember where you were and where you left off.

> I then found myself pregnant and hoped I'd be able to get it out of the way before the baby was born, but didn't. I did get quite a lot done when she was tiny, complicated too by the fact that I had spent the latter couple of months of pregnancy in and out of hospital. I was lucky in that Jane was an extremely easy and good baby and did always sleep in the early afternoons so I could put her down at twelve and she probably wouldn't wake until about a quarter to three, so I used to aim to get a couple of hours work done then. But, of course, once I'd got her it was much more difficult to get into the library. I could only do it on the odd Saturday. And then, by the time she was two-ish I did find myself saying, far too much 'Not now darling; I'm busy'; and I was thinking 'Heavens, I couldn't manage even the amount I'm doing with a second child' – we didn't want too long a gap between children. So, finally I did think, 'Well blow this for a lark'. It's a pity really because I have put quite a lot into it, but this is going to have to be shelved until I've got no children under five.

> I tried to have child-minding arrangements for one day a week. That wasn't very successful. And I also tried to have my husband home one day a week because I had great difficulty working in odd moments. I only had brief periods in the day when I was free. So I thought if I had one or two days a week when I knew I could sit down and work that would be much better. In fact all the arrangements I tried fell through in the end.

ER. What went wrong with them? Do you remember?

Well other things would happen. There would be a crisis, or something I had to do, hospital visit, seeing somebody, somebody would be coming round, so the times tended to get lost. And I didn't work very much in the evenings, largely because I used the evenings to compensate for not working during the day. I go out a lot in the evenings – meetings and things.

A very different outlook came from a woman whose children were of school age and who gave up study for a whole range of reasons (including dissatisfaction with her supervision, that she had a responsible and demanding job, and that she had taken on a time-consuming position in the community) but not because of her domestic ties.

My family have been very supportive; and I'm quite good at organizing things. I think – I hope anyway – that they haven't really suffered. My husband is very helpful, but not very good domestically. But they always had clean shirts, there was always a meal on the table when there should, and we didn't run out of sugar and dog-meat and things. The home was running quite smoothly. I got help in the home once I started earning, so that one burden was removed.

There were other complications, too, when, for example, the husband moved jobs, so that the wife moved away from the university at which she was doing her research, and, in addition, found herself coping with the removal and setting-up a new home, perhaps doing up an old house.

Why do these cases occur? To argue as some feminists would, that they are entirely the result of a male-dominated society, and would disappear if male dominance were broken, may, or may not be true. At the other extreme, it is only too easy to dismiss such cases as being further examples of the lack of foresight and planning, or even of excessive optimism, that can lead to theses dragging on. Some thought they would have the thesis finished before the child was born, misjudging yet again the amount still to be done, but also trusting to luck, or showing ignorance, in gambling on the pregnancy being an easy one. Others thought it would be fairly easy to continue their studies. As one said: 'I assumed that you could in fact sit at home and write when you had small children around, which you can't, or I couldn't.' Perhaps in some cases starting a family is sub-consciously a way out of research with which the student could not cope. One respondent, who might have hidden in this way behind her child, was adamant that her dropping of her research degree was due solely to her inadequacies, but few of us have the courage that enables us to look at our shortcomings that frankly.

There are basically two points that stand out here. The first is that, for the married woman intending to start a family, it is best, for various reasons, some of them medical, not to postpone this too long; and so, for her, the starting of a family becomes the extra difficulty that makes faltering research stop, just as the need to get a job often brings to an end the uncompleted research of the single woman or the man.

The second point is that for a woman who knows that she will before long want to start a family, it makes better sense to postpone the research and to use postgraduate study later as a means of bringing herself up-to-date, before re-entering employment. At present, however, the facilities for such re-entry are rarely available; though they ought to be, on a large scale.

For the men, as I said above, it is the combination of needing to put in a lot of time on a new job when the grant runs out and the demands of their families on their time that is often blamed for the decision to give up the thesis, or for just sliding into stopping work. I shall look at this below. But there is one separate and distinct category to look at here — those students who already had a job and a family when they started their postgraduate studies, and studied, mainly or wholly, part-time.

Though such students may be held to know that their studies would mean they would have less time for their families, knowing something is not the same as experiencing it. Their problem was in maintaining the determination, with which they had started, that they could put their families in second place during their free time.

ER. What view does your wife take of all the time this is taking?

Fortunately she's a very tolerant lady anyway. She was fully behind me. She felt that, if this was what I wanted to do then she would help me as much as she could. Relations didn't get very strained. She was very upset, as I was, when I came back and I said 'Oh hear. I've got to rewrite'. and so on. But again, I think, had she said to me at the time 'Oh, well, tell them to go to hell. Forget about it' I probably would have done; but fortunately she had the presence of mind to say 'Ah well. Come on. It's only 10,000 words. Damn it, you've written 60,000. You can knock up another 10,000 from somewhere'. She's been marvellous, she really has.

ER. How old are your kids?

The kids get fed up. Stuart is eleven and my daughter's six. He was quite proud when his dad came home with these books from the printers, and there was his dad's name on it. All these words in it. He thought it was tremendous. Yes, I think they feel neglected a bit.

One can feel very guilty if one sometimes says 'To hell with it. I'm taking the kids out', if one meets one's obligations there.

ER. You probably feel equally guilty if you are not taking them out.

Exactly. This is the problem. I think the PhD — if and when — will be a PhD in guilt.

ER. How has your wife taken this long period of your going over to S... and so on?

I would say in general she has hated it; but she has, I think, done her best to support me, just waiting for it to be over. Over the last year or so, when she's seen some light at the end of the tunnel, she's got much keener on the whole thing, basically, I think, because she wants it over with, and I sympathize with this view. I realize that it has intruded awfully at times on our private life. To be honest, if I hadn't felt that it was going to intrude to what to me was an unacceptable extent, I would have done much more work at home, because it would have got it over with much, much quicker.

ER. Was the alternative that you worked here later, or that you just didn't do it?

Just didn't do it. basically.

EMPLOYMENT

The data in Chapter 1 show that few students now complete both their research and their writing up before their studentships come to an end. Some may then be found further support, for perhaps as much as another year, by their department; and they may not have finished even at the end of that. Most go into employment almost immediately the studentship ends, and many of those I interviewed spoke of the difficulty of continuing their writing-up then. (Those students who had been studying part-time throughout their postgraduate studies had, of course, been meeting this difficulty throughout.) Here is what seems at first to be a simple example:

> At the end of my first year in teaching, at the end of my probationary year, I was made head of the newly formed Social Science Department, and then, two terms after that, I was promoted again and made deputy director of the sixth form. It meant I had tremendous amounts of work and responsibility spilling over from the school which was, I think, a major factor in my simply not having the time to devote to it. And also in my first year they gave me six entirely different subjects to teach in the school, so my preparation was enormous.

But under this apparently straight-forward and convincing account of why the student could not find time to complete a thesis there are further complications which emphasize the need not to be deceived by a superficially convincing explanation. The student had other ways of spending spare time, including very active and time-consuming participation in a local organization, which were not dropped because of the pressure of work. Also discontent with the postgraduate study, especially its teaching and supervision, was mentioned, and must have influenced the decision to drop the studies rather than other activities. And there were probably other reasons too, such as the diminishing relevance of a postgraduate qualification to a successful career in school-teaching.

Another example of the underlying complexity is a student who considered, after her grant ran out, living on social security in order to complete her thesis, but because the chance of a university or polytechnic job seemed slim, decided instead to be trained as a teacher, and then found that having worked for a PhD was a disadvantage − interviewing committees were afraid she would not be able to teach her subject at the level her pupils would need. Thus much of the incentive to finish the PhD had gone. Nevertheless she said she had intended to put some of her spare time into finishing it.

> When I started teaching this was my idea but I found I just couldn't make it. I couldn't do both things properly. I enjoy teaching in school and part of my enjoyment is doing the job properly, doing it thoroughly; and the first three or four years you do have to work pretty hard in preparation and marking and so on; and by the time the holidays came round I was usually in need of a week's rest; and then, when one week had gone, I would think 'I've got a few things to prepare for next term' and I'd spend a few days on that, and I might be left with, say, at Christmas or Easter, a week to get on with my thesis. Well, in the first couple of years, I did do

that. I spent some time in the Christmas, Easter and summer holidays on the thesis, but progress was so slow that it seemed that that would not be a way of completing it, that it would be impossible with weeks here and weeks there; and my original hope that after the first year of teaching I might be able to work on it evenings and in the holidays proved just impossible for me. I think if I'd been ruthless about school and stopped at 4 I could have done a lot more on the thesis; but I'm not that sort of person.

It is not only school-teachers who meet this difficulty. Here are some quotations from someone in industry:

There's no point in starting something at 9.30 that you know is going to take you four hours to complete unless you plan to go to bed at 2 o'clock because you know you're going to have to clear up half way through and start again the following night, but, on the other hand, if there is something that's going to take an hour or an hour and a half, then obviously it's worth doing.
     ER. Have you actually done anything on it at all in the last year or so?
     Virtually nothing.
     ER. What do you think you'd have to do to really get it going?
     Force myself basically to get home at 6.30 in the evening; sit down after supper at 8 o'clock and work until midnight six nights a week or something.
     ER. What about week-ends?
     That's a great idea if the remainder of the family will allow me to do so. But with young children I think that will be fairly difficult to do, if you are talking about day-time at the week-end, as opposed to the evening.

Another student, who had completed his thesis, described the amount of time this had taken:

I have put in every summer holiday, and every Easter holiday, and every Christmas holiday, for the last seven or eight years of my time on it. But, apart from the fact that I would rather have been doing other things, because it has been very hard work on top of a full teaching commitment, yes, I've quite enjoyed the writing up, I must say that.

Some students spoke of the difficulty of concentrating on the writing of the thesis in the evening after spending the day on demanding and exacting work. They said that by then they were too tired to concentrate. This is understandable. However, large numbers of theses are completed each year by students who have been finishing them in their evenings after a hard day's work, so clearly this is not impossible, and we have to ask why some can do it and others cannot? The answer is probably that those students who succeed in writing up while doing a full day's work, in spite of the demands of their families, are, on the one hand, those who have been successful in their research and have their notes well organized, so that the writing up is a relatively easy procedure, and, on the other hand, those who have a clear understanding of their subject, so that, again, writing up comes easily to them. It is significant that those students who mentioned the difficulty of concentration after a day's work also mentioned other difficulties.

Another student had a different problem:

I found it difficult to combine work − waitressing and so on − with working on the thesis. For a start, my creativity is erratic, and it's rather difficult to explain to Trust House Forte that you're onto a good scene this week and you don't want to work. (Note: this student had completed)

Another problem affected those students who, when they gave up the idea of being university teachers, decided to follow careers involving taking professional examinations in, say, accountancy or actuarial work, for which they had to study in their spare time, suspending the work on their theses. One said that he was about to take his last exam and would then resume the thesis; but a thesis that is set aside in this way is apt not to be taken up again, especially when, as so often, it is after all irrelevant to the student's career.

The need for most graduates to move home when taking a new job produced another kind of difficulty in continuing the thesis. The student then no longer has easy access to supervisors, the laboratory, the library, or, even more important today, to the computer in which he has stored his data and whose programming package he has learnt to use.

ER. How often did you manage to get over there?

About twice a year, I should think. I kept in touch via the phone, and that sort of thing. But, again, it just wasn't possible. If you're working full-time, you can't do it.

As I said above, this problem also hits married women when their husbands change jobs. One respondent was, understandably, bitterly resentful of having been obliged to move around.

Another student said:

One of the problems was, having left, I found this mistake in the programs, so I had to re-do the analysis, which took me a full summer, in S... and a lot of computer time. The annoying thing was it's the type of work you could do in term-time, but I can't transfer the material from S... to here.

The stress now being placed on schemes for combining research training with a job makes of wider interest what would otherwise be an individual and specialized case of conflict between the job and the research. A respondent had noticed a methodological article that she thought was relevant to her work. Her employers agreed that she should try to adapt this methodology to the study of some of their problems, and the author of the article suggested that she register for a higher degree so that he could help her with this. However, there were difficulties in the application of the methodology, which, while not, perhaps, insuperable, were certainly intractable, and the pressure of other work meant that the attempt had to be abandoned.

On the other side of the balance is a student who gained a university job, and although he, too, found that the preparation of courses, etc. made him give up the writing of his thesis for the first year or so, he resumed it on being told that his department would take into account his progress towards his PhD when deciding whether to recommend he be given tenure. However, of several university teachers in my sample, he was the only one who said he was being pressed by his department to complete. Most said that now they had university posts the PhD seemed unnecessary. The many polytechnic teachers were rather similar, though two reported they were being pressed by their department heads to do some consecutive research instead of bits of this and that.

An extra problem in finishing the writing up part-time affects students working in fields of knowledge that are changing and growing rapidly. Right up to the time when the thesis is finally handed in for typing, the student is expected to read everything published that is relevant to his research, adding to his literature survey where necessary, and also making appropriate changes to his own findings and conclusions. For the full-time student in some branches of, for example, aeronautical engineering, electronic engineering or computing, this can take up a substantial amount of the week. For the student who has taken a job and is trying to complete his thesis in his spare time, or for the one who has studied part-time throughout, the amount of time needed may exceed the total he has available. It is like running up a down escalator; a substantial effort is needed just to stay in the same place, while running quite fast can produce only a slow advance.

A similar hazard in these fields is that the student's own results become increasingly out-of-date.

> One of the difficulties particularly in electrical engineering is that it is such a rapidly advancing field that, had I been starting on the day I finished, we wouldn't have done it in the same way. And in particular there'd be one or two microprocessors in it, whereas it was then all being built with hardware, so to alter things you had to actually rewire them, whereas nowadays you'd build it so that to alter things you'd just be reprogramming. So it wasn't that there was some really fantastic discovery that had been made that had to be written up.

LONELINESS

In my earlier study of current graduate students (Rudd 1975) the loneliness of the graduate student's life was mentioned frequently by the students we interviewed. As it would be reasonable to expect this to influence dropping-out, I was watching for any indication of it in this present study. However, only five students mentioned it in relation to their social life and friendships — a number spoke of the solitary nature of the work, but that is to a large extent a separate issue, which will be discussed below. Of the five, one said quite explicitly: 'I learnt a lot about myself because it was a lonely and depressing time.' She spoke of the feeling that if she could get through that she could get through anything. Two had changed universities and found it took some time to make new friends; two, who stayed at the same university, said their friends had left; and two were out of the country for a long period doing field-work.

Most of the students had many friends, though generally not among their fellow graduate students.

By and large I found other research students fairly dull. A lot of them seemed to me to be doing things which were absolutely pointless.

FINANCE

Four kinds of financial problem were mentioned to me as having been relevant to the student either spending abnormally long on his studies or giving up:

a Inability to get a research council (or comparable) grant at all.
b Inability to get a grant for all of the three years for which support for a PhD is normally available.
c A grant had been held for three years, but too little progress had been made by the end of the three years for the student then to complete his thesis in his spare time, so that he sought support for a further period of full-time study.
d The student's difficulties in managing on his grant, or the attraction of more money elsewhere contributed to the decision to give up full-time study.

Those who cannot get a grant at all are unlikely to start postgraduate study, and so only five such cases turned up in my sample. This seemed unimportant to two of them, one having an adequate investment income, and one being a member of a well-paid profession who was able to support himself by a little part-time work. In neither of these cases was lack of money an important reason for giving up. Of the remaining three, two had relatively weak first degrees and had been, in every sense, struggling towards research degrees while supporting themselves from a variety of jobs. One had gained a full-time job teaching in higher education and seemed to think he was still working for the higher degree for which his registration had long lapsed. The other was a 'mature' student and was still living a hand-to-mouth existence, partly supported by his wife, and fully intending that he, his wife and family would continue to make substantial sacrifices until he had completed his thesis.

The fifth of the students without a grant had a strange and complicated story of application forms not sent out at the right time or by the right people. There seemed to have been misunderstandings, and it was possible that a university teacher had simply forgotten to deal with some administrative work. After being supported by family for two terms, the student was continuing research part-time without being registered for a degree, but was about to go to a different university for a taught course, which he completed successfully.

Three students had been unable to gain support for a third year. In one case this was the result of the procedures for allocating studentships that the SSRC was following at the time. The student had a lectureship at a university and might possibly still complete her PhD – though, as she was publishing books and articles, this seemed unimportant. The second had previously completed a masters degree with support from a source other than a research council, and neither he nor anyone concerned with this case at his university had realized that this precluded a third year of support from a research council. The third had followed a mathematics degree by a one-year training in statistics, and so was also ineligible for support for more than two years of the PhD. For both these students the lack of further money was a major factor in the decision to give up. The Swinnerton-Dyer Working Party (ABRC 1982) has recommended that, in certain cases of this kind, students should be given further support by the research councils.

In the third category, where students' financial problems arose from their having made too little progress in the first three years of research, lack of money was in no way responsible for the lack of progress, though lack of money to continue studying full-time beyond their three years can sometimes, as I have said above, contribute to a student who had made too little progress in the earlier stages eventually deciding to give up.

Three students said they had not been able to manage on their grants and had got into debt, and another said that the attraction of more money in a job was one factor in his decision to give up fairly early in his research. One of these, having interpolated periods of employment as a research assistant between periods of grant, was well on the way to submitting his thesis and has since gained a PhD. The others had given up, but in each case the lack of money was a minor factor and it was quite clear that, even with a larger grant, they would still not have completed.

It therefore seems that, except where a grant was not available for the third year of research, the lack of finance, though it undoubtedly prevents students starting postgraduate study, and undoubtedly delays some, had little place amongst the substantial reasons for the students I saw giving up. Since then various changes may have increased the number giving up for this reason.

RUNNING A BUSINESS
I have already said that two students mentioned having patented inventions. Both had set up companies. One seemed well set on his way to completing his PhD. Both had intended that their firms should take up very little of their time, but the second student's plans went awry and he found that his business was indeed taking a large proportion of the time he should have been spending on his research. Although this was not the only reason he did not complete his PhD it seemed the most influential. At the time of the interview his firm was both flourishing and growing; and although subvention in the form of a studentship is a somewhat unusual way for the state to aid the establishment of a science-based manufacturing firm, I felt that neither society nor the student had lost anything from his not having a PhD.

Another student, while studying for a taught masters degree, had set up a small business connected with his academic interests. Although, in our discussion, he stressed other reasons for his failure to gain his degree, blaming bad teaching, it seemed likely that, in his case too, the business was absorbing his time and energy to an extent that affected his academic work.

THE LACK OF UNIVERSITY JOBS
Many of my informants had thought that if they entered postgraduate study they were on the road to a university career:

I'd just assumed that if I got my PhD then I would get an assistant lectureship, and that's it, I would be in a university for the rest of my life.

Not surprisingly, then, a number of respondents said that one influence on their decision to abandon their attempt to gain a higher degree was that the chances of a university job were becoming slim. For example, one student, speaking of 'the contraction of the university job market' said:

> When I started doing research this was a tiny cloud on the horizon. Two years later it was very clear that that was what was going to happen, and the THES were already saying, in my second year of research, that the job market was going down and down and down; and it was getting more and more complicated. And I remember reading the THES and looking at their statistics on how many Oxbridge graduates were getting jobs, how many others if you had a first or second class degree, and thinking then, well maybe I've got as good a chance as anybody, but it was already down to three to two against as it were. That was the reason for changing.

Another said:

> If I'd realized at University that there was virtually no chance of getting a job once you'd got your PhD I'd have really thought twice about doing it at all because that was as much as anything why I got out, when I got to ... and saw the number of people who were leaving there either to go on the dole or do something completely different.

Perhaps I should again add that, in all these cases, there were other reasons for giving up. If the student had been completely enjoying what he was doing and had seen the way forward to the PhD as a clear easy path, he would have completed it, even though he was looking for a job outside higher education. However, given that there were other difficulties, the decision not to stay in academic life overrode any incentive to overcome them.

7

Research Problems

The difficulties with their postgraduate studies that led to students failing to complete them within a reasonable time do not all fall neatly into categories. It may sometimes be possible to say, unequivocally, that the research has gone wrong because the initial choice of topic was bad, being unsuitable for any research student, or for this student, or, though this student might reasonably have been expected to manage it, being one that he has handled incompetently; but the explanation is more likely to come into a grey area between these, where they overlap or shade into one another and where the amount of emphasis placed on any one element in an interacting combination of causes is highly debatable. For analysis, one needs to categorize these difficulties and mistakes, and so, in this chapter and the one that follows it, I try to look separately at each of the main ways in which the students' research and studies go wrong. It remains essential for the reader to bear in mind that I am simplifying a complex interrelation of causes and effects. In particular, any one kind of mistake, failure or disaster is apt to have a domino effect, causing other things to go wrong, if only because more time spent on any one item means less for others.

EARLY DECISIONS
It is well known that if anything can go wrong there is a high probability that it will, and so each decision made opens up the possibility of a mistake. For postgraduate students, the first error can be the initial decision to be a postgraduate student at all, which I discussed in Chapter 3 and to which I shall be returning in Chapter 11. The next decision is between research and a taught course − this is not a sharp division into two categories, but more a matter of where the balance lies − and I have too little information on how this decision was taken to discuss it in detail. After this, for research students, comes the choice of a university, a subject on which to do research, and a more detailed topic within that subject; the order in which these decisions are taken varies from student to student. For taught-course students, the choices at this stage are between universities, etc., and also between courses; later they will have to make the same choice of a research topic since nearly all courses include a research project. Of the few taught-course students I interview, nearly all fell down at the research project stage, and so what I have to say about problems in research applies, *mutatis mutandis*, to them too,

and I shall be discussing their problems in research alongside those of other students doing research.

CHOICE OF A UNIVERSITY
Some students first decide at which university or universities they would like to study, and then decide on the subject for their research. A variant of this arises where a science or engineering department arranges a series of presentations at which members of staff tell their third-year students about the opportunities of doing research with them − they are saying to the students 'You should do research and do it here. Choose from amongst the topics we can offer you.'

Others decide on what they wish to do their research and then try to discover where they can work on their chosen topic, using such sources of information as the advice of the staff teaching them for their first degree, the authorship of published articles, and the British Library's publication, *Research in British Universities, Polytechnics and Colleges*. It is the first of these sources of information that they use most, especially in the arts, and given the impossibility of any member of the teaching staff knowing who in his field is doing research on what at every university, it is not surprising that the advice is not invariably accurate.

Perhaps one should regard discovering where to go for postgraduate study as the first test of a vocation for research; the student who cannot do the small piece of research needed accurately to discover such a vital piece of information has no flair for research and should not be doing it. Unfortunately it is not as simple as that. The staff probably think they are helping students to make a rational and informed choice; but from the student's viewpoint it can look a little different.

> We all went to see supervisors and they say 'What do you want to do?' You say 'I don't know really' and they say 'Well, how about doing something like this; I have an interest in this'. and so you say 'Yes', but you don't understand a word they're saying; it's way over your head. You get a vague idea of what it involves, but it's not really until one gets into it that one really knew what they'd planned.

The student with a first who fails this test is still going to do research, but will do it badly in the wrong place. Also the third-year undergraduate cannot be expected to know how anxious many departments are to attract potentially good students, and that this sometimes leads them to give too rosy a picture of their ability to ensure that a student working in a particular area will have the necessary facilities and be supervised by someone with sufficient knowledge of the field. Moreover, it is especially difficult for a student to discover whether, at a particular university,his supervision will have all the qualities that the combination of his own needs and his subject call for − this involves the departmental ethos and procedures as well as the qualities and attitudes of the supervisor.

CHOICE OF A TOPIC
The choice of topic is often the most difficult decision facing any student whose higher degree requires some research, but especially the PhD student.

The topic must be one that the student finds interesting so that he will enjoy working on it. It must be just the right size to be completed in the time and with the resources available. It must offer scope for original research, but, at the same time, the student and his supervisor need to know in advance that the problem to be tackled is soluble. There is an unavoidable difficulty here; it is impossible to be sure that a problem can be solved, that a given piece of research will produce results, until this has been done. But if it has been done already, the research is not original. What the supervisor and student are seeking, therefore, is a topic which, while it has not already been studied, is sufficiently like others that have been studied for them to feel confident that success is possible. The closer the new topic lies to earlier work the greater the certainty that it can be tackled, but the less the original contribution.

It is probable that much of the explanation of the differences between fields in their success rates lies here; those fields in which the student's work is likely closely to resemble other previous work have the highest success rates.

If there is an ideal way for a student to choose a research topic, I would not, of course, expect to find it amongst my sample. They did, however, show that it is possible here to go wrong in two opposite directions; almost all of those for whom the choice of a topic was a relevant factor had settled on it either very quickly or very slowly.

Those who chose a topic quickly settled on it in one of two ways. A few had done some form of undergraduate project in the area and wished to go further with it, an approach which has substantial advantages − problems seem more likely to arise where the student chooses a topic about which he knows little. More commonly, however, the idea came from the supervisor. Occasionally, the student knew he wanted to work in a given area and went to see someone who specialized in the chosen field and who suggested a topic. More often, the supervisor had the research topic ready and sought a student, either by the kind of departmental open-day that I have already mentioned, or by approaching an individual third-year undergraduate. One student said that immediately after the board of examiners decided he would be given a first, but before the publication of the list that told him his result, a number of members of staff approached him about the possibility of his doing research under their supervision.

It is, by the way, a fallacy to believe that the arts student finds his own topic and the science student has his suggested to him; examples of both approaches can be found in both fields. The difference is one of balance; a higher proportion of arts students find their own topic.

There is no reason to expect projects that are the brain-child of a supervisor always to be successful. Moreover, I cannot be sure how often the failure of those that were described to me was due to the research topic being in some way unsuitable for research students, or to the inadequacies of the student. What the students told me was often, however, far more revealing than they realized, and helped me form some kind of judgement.

In some cases I would guess that the basic problem was the inadequacy of the student, but in other cases it seemed likely that the often highly able students I was interviewing were justified in saying that the problems on which they were working could not be solved within the time available to a research student. The differences between supervisors lie in how they cope with such a situation. In many fields a good researcher is like a good leader of mountain walkers; he always has a number of alternative plans in his head and if he cannot follow his chosen route will take one of the others. That some supervisors had not turned onto alternative approaches or alternative projects their students who were working unsuccessfully on topics that the supervisors had proposed, may imply (a) that the supervisors were not good at either supervision or research, or (b) that an attempt to turn the students onto other paths had not worked — perhaps they were not up to the task or rejected the supervisors' advice — or (c) that the students were working in a field, or a department, in which it was not expected that they would complete their theses quickly. Of these three possibilities, the third, as it relates to collective, rather than individual, attitudes to the way research students should do their research and should be supervised, will be left to a later chapter.

One explanation of some of these cases was that the student, in deciding that certain work could not be carried further, or that a given approach to a problem was inappropriate, was not merely going against the supervisor's wishes and advice, but rejecting an approach to which the supervisor was committed, and so criticizing the validity of the supervisor's own work. Here is part of a student's account of his attempt to build on some work that his supervisor had done or supervised over a longish period.

> The research was boiled down really to trying to find out why certain things didn't happen. This, in hindsight, is not a good subject to do research on. But also a thesis had been written on it about ten years ago, and one of my difficulties was that I really couldn't (a) find any extra experimental evidence anyway, and (b) I found it impossible to reproduce some of the alleged results from the previous thesis anyway.

In another case, the student decided that he was being expected to adopt a psychological approach to what were basically pharmaecological problems, and rejected that approach.

In another case the research topic proposed by the supervisor was simply too ambitious. The supervisor was newly arrived from a senior position in industry, and misjudged the amount a PhD student could do given the resources of a university department.

As I said above, some students had taken a substantial time to fix on a topic; if a student who has three years in which to do a piece of research spends a year or more deciding on what he will do it, he either has to work very fast in his remaining time or he is not going to complete it. One student, on being asked, some eight years after he first started his PhD, at what point his choice of a research topic was cut and dried, replied 'I'm still not sure that it *is* cut and dried.' I put to another student, as a summary of what he had said, for confirmation, that he had started by casting about widely and had then spent a year or so looking around. He replied,

> Yes, very much encouraged by Brian, who thought it was very important not to choose something too soon if I was going to have to live with it for a number of years.

Another, who started and abandoned a series of different projects, spoke of a total lack of any sense of urgency in the choice of a project. He saw himself as at the beginning of a life-time's career in the academic world, so there was no need for haste.

A mathematician said:

> I think the basic problem was that I didn't have a particular topic and my supervisor did not say, for better or worse, until the second year, 'I think that is the problem you want and I want you to do this'. He said to me 'Look around. Do whatever you fancy'. So he didn't push me into a particular area; so I was doing bits and pieces.

Here is another fairly typical description of this process from a literature student:

> Having made the decision to do some research, I went and talked it over with the chap who's now my supervisor; and he said 'Yes. Go ahead. Excellent idea. Let's find a topic', which was crazy, stupid. He didn't have lists of topics up his sleeve at the time; he may have now, but he didn't then. So I cast around and thought of some ideas and we tossed them around in a very amateurish way, because neither of us really knew whether they were worth researching — obviously you can't do, can you, until they've been researched out? And I don't think he had sufficient knowledge to be able to say whether they were likely to be fruitful or not, and so we guessed at a few topics and I started on one that seemed fairly broad and interesting, and found in fact that it wasn't at all broad and interesting. And so this shifted, and shifted again, and shifted again. I spent a year shifting really, until in the end I found a topic that I'm perfectly satisfied with. I think it's a very valuable contribution actually, but it took a year to get there.

There is a difficult and inescapable dilemma here. It is important that the student should take a major part in the choice of a topic, rather than having one thrust at him, both because the selection and delineation of a research topic is an important part of the process of research that the student is learning, and also so that he can be sure it is one that suits him. It is also important that he should adequately explore the possibilities and the implications of his choice and, though an experienced supervisor can help keep down the time this takes, it may still be a lengthy process. What is needed, then, is some procedure that allows the student adequate time for the choice of a topic without cutting into the time available for the research itself. I shall return to this issue when putting forward solutions to the various problems I have found in the present study.

Another characteristic of a satisfactory research topic is that it is one on which the student can be supervised — a student who tries to work on a topic remote from the expertise of everyone in his chosen department is asking for trouble. It is in this context that a whole set of problems were caused by a government research organization giving out money for research in a particular field without checking that the university departments it chose were fully competent to do the research. The funds included money for research students who then set out on research projects in which they were not going to be properly supervised.

RESEARCH THAT CROSSES DISCIPLINARY BOUNDARIES

The question of adequate supervision is related to another which concerns students in certain subjects — notably education and geography — which draw on the theories, techniques and skills of a range of disciplines. The research student in geography may not have anyone in his own department who is competent to help him over a particular problem, but there may be someone who could do so in a department of economics, or statistics, or sociology, or botany. The first hurdle in front of students and their supervisors in such areas is to recognize that they in fact have a problem with which they need help — they may know too little about the subject on which they are working even to recognize the nature of their problems or the extent of their ignorance, and even when they do, admitting to ignorance does not come easy to everyone. After that, they need to identify where they can get help, which, within the departmental structure of most universities, is not easy. Then they have to arrange for help, and those who are expected to help can be forgiven for being reluctant to find the very substantial amount of time that is occasionally needed: when, for example, the student's first degree has not provided an adequate background for what he is trying to do. Further, the member of staff may well feel that the geographer, educationist or whatever he may be, has, through ignorance, taken on a research problem that is beyond him, so that time spent helping him is largely wasted.

A related problem arises where a student, in a department whose subject has more precise boundaries, decides to work on a topic that crosses disciplinary boundaries. But in such cases this is more likely to be recognized from the beginning and it is therefore more likely that appropriate arrangements for joint supervision, or at least advice, will be made. What marks out such subjects as geography, education and librarianship is the frequency with which they do cross boundaries, the likelihood that they will cross them in several directions in the same research, and perhaps that they will have less recognition of their own limitations.

It is possible that I am singling out geography, education and librarianship in this way because I know far more about how some of their students should have been doing their research than I would know in the case of students in, say, biology, and I can therefore comment on difficulties of which I heard from the students, but of which they themselves were, in many cases, unaware.

The problem certainly spreads far more widely. A study by the Science Policy Research Unit at the University of Sussex of the scheme for interdisciplinary studies fostered jointly by the SERC and SSRC (Joint SERC-SSRC Committee 1983) found that students on the scheme frequently reported problems of supervision. There does, however, seem to me to be a major difference between, on the one hand, these subjects which straddle many fields, drawing on the findings, ideas, theories and methodology of others without having much of a discipline of their own, and, on the other hand, cases where a subject has an overlap with a limited number of other subjects, as economic history overlaps with economics and history, or where there is no overlap but the student does work that crosses the frontier — when, for example, the study of a poet leads to a study of his relationship with a new school in art, and so into the history of art.

Even in these reasonably clearly defined cases of the crossing of boundaries, however, the informality of the arrangements for supervision, and their lack of structure, can still result in the student making no contact with a member of staff with related interests in another department.

FAILURE TO ACHIEVE RESULTS

Although some topics in my sample seemed ill-chosen in that, at least with hindsight, one could say that it ought to have been seen at the outset that a PhD student could not be expected to achieve results in three years, there were other topics not so obviously doomed to failure on which the student nevertheless achieved no results. An example is a geologist who was doing his field-work overseas in an area where it seemed likely there would be work still to be done, though it was chosen more for the student's convenience than for its potential for research. He had difficulty in obtaining rock specimens, though he did find some which he got back to his university, where he

> did some lab work which I thoroughly enjoyed; but the results were so inconclusive that I would have had to start again. It wasn't as if I could say of that tiny little chunk that I'd done well, these specimens show a trend in such and such a direction. They couldn't. There was nothing, absolutely nothing, to work on that I could see getting bigger and bigger.

There were a number of such cases, where students told me their research was unsuccessful. In addition, in some of the cases where students told me they had not completed the writing up, they may well have doubted whether they really had enough results, had collected enough material, or in other ways had achieved enough, to gain their degrees.

Failure to get results is more clear-cut in the sciences than in some other fields — a chemical engineer doing a theoretical study for which he needed stable equations, whereas all his equations proved unstable, had virtually no thesis at all. The equivalent in history is the student who finds too little material in the archives on which he is working. As one of them put it:

> It was perhaps a strategic mistake to have chosen this topic or be pushed into it. The material is very diverse; there's nothing concrete. There has been tremendous difficulty in marrying it. You dredge through thousands and thousands of things and you might find a bit of gold here and there, if you're lucky. There's never been anything substantial that you have in a block that you can put together that has a coherency and theme.

In literature, the equivalent is perhaps the student who fails to find anything new and important to say about his chosen author, but here the failure to get results is less clear cut; the student in literature can always find something to say, whether this makes any contribution to scholarship or not.

I cannot, without risking a breach of confidence, report much of the many long and detailed accounts students gave me of their failure to get results. I shall try, however, to pick out families of problems. Before doing this, though, I should point out that failure is rarely total and final; it almost always seems possible that a little more work, a few more experiments, will produce the elusive success. For a few of the students I interviewed, that success had indeed come before I saw them.

> I had in fact decided that I wasn't going to do it and had everything packed up in a room, and my supervisor rang me up last July and said 'You've got one more year to write up; why don't you?' and I said 'Well I'm completely stuck on this' and he said I must really sort it out if I'm going to write up at all, and we managed to get it sorted out.

There were, however, several families of problems that cropped up with more than one student:

1 The student's mathematical ability was too slight for the research in which he was engaged. This could be a sub-set of the wider problem of the student starting on a problem that does not match his abilities, skills and training, or it could be a reflection of the weakness of our teaching of mathematics to non-mathematicians. This difficulty was especially common.

2 Basic and major problems in the computer software meant that the student had to devote so much time to getting his material into the computer, or getting bugs out of the computing, that he had too little time for the rest of his research.

3 The opposite problem — the student became so addicted to computing that it became an end in itself instead of a means to an end, and so much time was spent on the elaboration of computing methods that too little other work was done.

4 The annual cycle in certain problems in biology. If the experiment of a chemist or a physicist fails he may simply repeat it, or repeat it in a modified form, or build a new piece of equipment. For some biologists, however, failure may mean the loss of an entire year while they wait for their plant to come back to the same point in the growing cycle, or their animal or fish to reach again the same point in the cycle of breeding. Most students learn through mistakes, but the biologist may simply not be able to afford to make any as the consequences are so serious. As one of them said:

> If you make a mistake in experimental design, and you do an experiment on mice which takes a month to complete, you just start again the next month. If you make a mistake in April or May on your lambs, you say 'What a pity, We'll try again next year.' which is slightly different.

5 The inability to make the jump from finding a practical solution to giving an account of its significance for the theory of the subject and incorporating it into the theory. Only a few students explicitly mentioned that they had this difficulty, but others gave accounts of their work that strongly suggested they found this step too difficult. They would say, for example, that they decided to spend the time improving the hardware rather than writing up for publication.

6 The discovery that someone else was working in the same area and further ahead.

THIRD PARTY RISKS

All these reasons for the failure to gain results (except, perhaps, the last) imply some weakness on the part of the student. There is another group of contributory reasons for failure which, except in as far as they reflect an unfortunate choice of topic, cannot be regarded as in any way the student's fault. They arise from the need, at some stage in the research, to gain some kind of permission, access or agreement from a government, or a civil service department, or some other body.

There are two potential problems here — that permission may be refused, and that the decision may take longer than the student can wait for it. It is a hazard especially for archaeologists wanting to dig overseas, and was a significant reason for one of them giving up. Another student gave up early the idea that she would do research in Zambia on realizing that, as she was born in what was then Rhodesia, she would, at that time, be *persona non grata*. A student of Russian literature who needed to do part of her research in the Soviet Union was about to go there when the vicissitudes of international relations brought student exchanges temporarily to an end. By the time the visa became available, not only was it too late, but the student had wasted a disastrous amount of time over the uncertainties of her position and the need to change plans. The Home Office took so long to consider an application to do research in a prison that it was too late for the student to do it. He had changed his topic so that he would no longer need their permission, but the waste of time was a factor in his not having completed.

Most of these difficulties would be covercome by my proposal, in Chapter 11, that students should do the planning of their research before they become full-time students. The time spent gaining persmission for it would then delay the start of full-time research, not its completion.

WRITING UP

The stage of the higher degree at which most students had given up, or over which they had spent very substantial amounts of time, was the writing up. There were two main difficulties at this stage: slowness in writing and an inability to bring their material into some form of coherent shape. Clearly, these two problems are not wholly separate — people whose ideas are clear and who have an overall shape firmly in their minds write more quickly. Also here, as elsewhere, motivation is relevant in some cases, and important in a few.

I cannot remember any of the students telling me that he wrote abnormally slowly, and when I asked any of them if they perhaps found it a little difficult to write rapidly, nearly all of them indignantly denied this. Perhaps slowness in writing is regarded as an inadmissible aspect of character, rather like the sea-sickness of which Jerome K. Jerome noted: 'It is a curious fact, but nobody ever is sea-sick — on land.' However, in some cases the facts spoke only too clearly for themselves, especially the length of time they had spent on the writing up.

One student who came near to an admission of difficulty in finding appropriate wording with facility and speed had, in fact, submitted a PhD dissertation after four years work on it, but had been failed by the examiners.

When discussing what he had gained from his period as a graduate student he said:

> I don't know whether people are born with the ability to express themselves clearly and precisely from the word go, but I certainly had problems with knowing to some degree what I wanted to say, and obviously you don't know what you're saying until you've said it, in the simplest way. I had a fair idea of what I wanted to say, but I couldn't get it down in terms that I felt would express it best. Although I wouldn't say I have reached the point where I can always invariably do that — I still have to think hard, and I still don't manage it entirely — certainly over the four years, as I got towards the end, my ability to express myself was stronger; and I think also it wasn't just the ability to express myself. I could work through from the vague idea to the clear formulation more quickly.

Another student saw his inability to get his thesis written, perhaps rightly, as a kind of work-block:

> I suppose I was reluctant to put pen to paper for anything that was going to be in the region of a final draft. I think I felt — and other people that were in a similar position to myself did seem to have — a kind of block against actually writing something down, which now, in retrospect, seems a little hysterical perhaps in some ways.

The students seemed far less inhibited about admitting that they had been held up, or stopped by, the difficulty of pulling together all their material. Typically, when telling me about this they would point with pride at their enormous collection of box-files, piled in a corner of the room or filling a long shelf.

This is largely, though not exclusively, a problem of the students in arts and social studies — there is more of a set pattern about the writing up of research in science and technology, which makes it easier for the student to 'Begin at the beginning, ... and go on till you come to the end: then stop'. The following extracts from students' comments on this problem come, in sequence, from a music student, a biologist, two historians, and three students working in different branches of literature. However, *mutatis mutandis*, such comments could come from virtually any subject.

> I think I was, earlier on, and perhaps even now, unable to differentiate between what was absolutely essential and what could be dispensed with. So my problem was really a sort of *embarras de richesse*. I mean, there was so much material and it all seemed fantastic. And I couldn't put it all in, but I tried to. And of course this made the whole thing of mammoth size, totally unwieldy. So I wish I had been taught more precisely how to be more discriminating with material.

> The major problem in the writing up was the organization of the material — a problem which I never solved.
>
> ER. Was it the larger scale, the problem of trying to write something much larger than the papers you were used to writing?

The scale would have been one problem, but the most important was the problem of ordering the material into some sort of logical sequence, which the work didn't follow, you see.

It was a very large topic with voluminous record sources, very much uncharted territory, on the one hand, and, on the other hand, the interaction between my changing interests and my material has meant I could have written my PhD several years ago, but I would not have been happy with what I would have produced. And what has happened is my expectations have continually run ahead of my ability to match them.

I wrote a series of sort-of short monographs. I did it area by area. This isn't what they wanted from the thesis, but it seemed to be quite reasonable. But I've never really combined these monographs into a real connecting thesis, and whenever I start it always fell to bits.

The whole thing was just much, much too big for a PhD thesis. There were three or four books there that I was struggling to get all compressed, and consequently sloppily, into one. I think perhaps that would have been apparent if I'd been writing more closely and carefully at first − I think that happened because the writing was sloppy, so was the way I was thinking.

I probably started researching the first chapter or something − probably the wrong place to start. And I should think I shifted again, and I just drifted on really. It only became clear to me after three years when I was actually writing it at the end of my formal three-year period; and it's only in the last two or three years that I've felt able to contain the whole thesis in my mind at once.

Unfortunately Bill saw my thesis in a socio-political concept. I saw my thesis in an intellectual history concept − history of thought − and Bill spent most of his time trying to get me to put in the social-economic-political background, and that's of course why it turned out to be two theses.

Naturally, one wonders how these students had got into this state, how they had come to amass material in a form in which they could not cope with it, and why they gave up at that stage when others persevered? The collection of material in a form in which it does not lend itself to easy use at this last stage is a failure of planning. It is the job of the supervisor to ensure that the student's research is properly planned; but it is difficult to see what he could in practice do about this. He could, and should, reiterate the need, when collecting any material, to consider the use to which it will be put, and to collect it in a form that will facilitate that use; but this is something which it is easier to accept intellectually than to put into practice. The form in which notes are kept is very much an individual matter, in most fields, the form being attuned to the way in which the individual's memory operates and the way in which he thinks.

However the notes are kept, this is still in many cases the most difficult stage, when the student has to stand back from his material, to think about it and to find a coherent pattern in it. There are differences between subjects here, which may account for the greater tendency of the arts and social sciences students to fail at this stage. The science student has to put more creative effort into the initial planning of his experiments, and so does the social scientist doing survey work. If the experiments or surveys are successful, much of the writing up can follow a set form, though there is still the need for original and creative thinking about the significance of the results to the development of theory. And some science and technology students have the difficult task of putting into words successful research that takes the form of a piece of hardware or a computer programme.

For the literature student, the earlier stages of magpie-like collection of material may be easier, but the time of reckoning comes when the writing up begins. Therefore it could be that at this stage there is more of a winnowing that separates those with the ability to write a thesis from the rest.

For many this stage of taxing toil seems far less enjoyable than what they have previously been doing, such as dilettante reading; though for those who are successful in writing up there are rewards in a sense of mastering new skills — stretching their wings — as well as the excitement of the new visions of the truth that come to them. Those who dismiss this stage as boring may not have given themselves the opportunity to discover what it is really like or may not have the ability to accept the challenges it offers — perhaps they would not succeed in gaining new skills and for them there are no new visions of the truth. In comments like that which follows they may merely be saying sour grapes, or they may, as they claim, be rebelling at an arid academic exercise. The first student quoted stopped work after the first term of his third year. He had written draft chapters as he went along, so that the stage at which he stopped was where he should have been turning his drafts into a coherent thesis that had something to say.

> ER. What made you give up at that point?
>
> Well, I was getting rather fed up with it. I'd done the interesting bit — the actual research work and the seeking of ideas — and I was coming to the point where you have to start writing footnotes, getting the whole thing into order, making sure you've read anything that any fool has ever written on the subject, all this kind of thing, and, rather than putting down your own ideas, starting to think how you can express things so that the professor won't immediately say you'll have to change it; and none of that appealed to me at all.

The following comment came from a student who had spent a long time trying, not very successfully, to write up his voluminous material, and whose draft had been with his supervisor for a substantial time.

> I don't really care that much about writing up my ideas. I enjoy the study and I enjoy talking about it, all of which I can do with students. The actual sitting down and going through what is after all a very laborious process, the real work of writing it, I don't find particularly rewarding; and I was for a long time playing with the feeling I'd learnt what I set out to learn, and getting the piece of paper at the end, which meant doing the work,

didn't really matter to me personally; and I'm not sure yet how true that is. I don't really know how disappointed I am in not finishing it.

There is about this comment a distinct flavour of rationalizing an inability to do something that was too difficult for him — a rationalization that is necessary for the preservation of the *amour propre* in the face of defeat.

THE INDIVIDUAL AND SEPARATE NATURE OF PhD WORK

How far the student feels alone and isolated in his research depends to a certain extent on his personality. Putting people together is no guarantee that they will establish satisfactory relationships, and even in group research, of which I will say more below, a student can feel very much on his own. But, even beyond this, there is an element in the very nature of academic research, and especially research for a higher degree, which tends to cut the individual off from those around him. Research has to be new and different from what has gone before. Generally, the further the student goes in it, the fewer are the people who know enough about it to discuss it with him on equal terms. This separation is increased by the natural wish of the researcher, and the requirement for the research student, to be able to say without challenge that his ideas and his work are his own.

Solitary work and intellectual isolation are, naturally, most common outside the laboratory sciences — in the arts and social sciences more of the work is done in the relative solitude of libraries. However, there is no sharp division of subjects into those where students work shoulder to shoulder and those where they are on their own. The social sciences, and increasingly the arts too, are beginning to use computers, which tend to bring students together. In certain sciences, especially biological and earth sciences, some work is done in the laboratory, but much of it is field work in which the student is on his own; and the mathematician is likely to work as much in isolation as the historian. Moreover, a student can be very much on his own in a laboratory, and, in the arts, if he shares a study-room, he may find the company of the others sharing it pressing in on him too much.

Nevertheless, it was mainly from humanities students that I heard comments such as:

> I also found that it was a very isolated existence, that I was working on this subject by myself, that I was therefore spending a lot of time in libraries and sitting in my own lodgings, spending in fact days on end without seeing anybody, and I found this rather depressing.

However, even from a psychology student — and in some universities psychology is part of the science faculty — I heard this comment:

> I think what I had missed was any sense of working with colleagues. Everything that could have happened to stop me working in a group happened.

A different point of view came from a history student, when he was asked about organized contact with other students.

My supervisor had monthly meetings of all his supervisees, which could range from three to about six depending on what we had been doing; but that was about all. He did have occasional parties, and there was a research group, a techniques group, run by Professor D..., which also brought people together, but that was about it. There wasn't very much contact.

ER. There wasn't any opportunity for casual interchange with other students where you could natter with each other about what you were doing?

Yes, there was; in the University Library. It wasn't in any sense a sort of defined form, but you did meet people there fairly constantly; and that was one of the things that got me down — constantly talking about what I'd discovered this morning.

There can be no doubt of the need to break through the students' intellectual isolation — not to make them happier but to give them perspective, to enable them to see their subjects in wider contexts, and to stop them becoming narrow and limited. The usual way that departments try to do this is by bringing students together for seminars.

It was the regular Friday evening seminar of staff and students in the social anthropology department to which I gave that particular paper — it seems that every social anthropology department has a Friday evening thing which is considered to be the event of the week — and whilst there were other students there — students who were around, who were back from their field-work, or not ready to go off — I would say that at least two-thirds of the people there were staff, and then there were also visiting scholars.

Friday is a popular choice for these gatherings, so that they can move to the pub for much of the evening without the next day's work suffering too much. In some ways, these informal gatherings in the pub, where students and staff talk shop as well as just chatting, are more valuable than the more formal sessions.

Where departments do not provide seminars, this is a matter of legitimate criticism from the students.

There was a total absence of seminars and so on which really would have enabled you to meet other people and talk theoretically about issues arising from research.

One student described a department in which, as there was no seminar provided, the students got together to organize their own. Like most student activities, this collapsed after a while; but two years later a new generation of students again started organizing their own seminar.

On the other hand, where seminars are provided, these are criticized too. The problem is partly the difficulty of ensuring that the seminars are brilliant and stimulating, partly the problem of pitching them at a level at which they will interest, and be intelligible to, those not working in the precise area covered but will not bore those with a more specific interest in it, and partly students' reluctance to spend time being broadened.

There was a research seminar which was organized by the professor where research students met, or were supposed to meet, once a fortnight, and one of them would discuss his work and progress, and the others would chip in with comments, but even at (this major university) the range of subjects was so large that really you were being asked to comment on areas of which you had no specialist knowledge at all, and in many cases, such as my own, not even the background knowledge other people had from their undergraduate days.

Also there are further problems when the seminar papers are given by the students themselves, such as the unwillingness of individual students to expose their work and ideas to potentially hostile criticism, especially at a formative stage. This was mentioned in the context of increased rivalry for jobs, and of the effect not only on discussion at seminars but also on more informal exchanges. I was told of an increasing unwillingness among students to help each other, and of a fear that other students at seminars would exploit any vulnerability in front of the staff, who would be giving references and wielded some patronage for jobs. One student said:

> Half the other thing about D..., of course, among research students at that stage, is that the whole thing is so bloody competitive, particularly with the feeling that jobs were drying up all over the place. Everyone felt they were competing against one another. There was this dreadful thing of an incredible reluctance to say anything in seminars; people were dreadfully inhibited from revealing themselves. And to some extent you do end up competing against these people — you keep seeing them at job interviews — and it's very difficult to know how to get past that.

SUMMING UP
This attempt to isolate the various academic problems associated with failure in postgraduate research, other than the problem of supervision, has, from its nature, been somewhat fragmentary. For the student, however, these problems come together and interact, often in very individual ways. To take a simple example, the student who cannot see how to bring his material into a shape and pattern is likely to feel the absence of opportunities to talk to fellow students about his research; and where there is little contact between students, the student is more likely to grow stale, and then to go through the motions of reading without absorbing what is being read.

Nearly all the cases that I heard about had this kind of complex set of interrelated causes of failure. Even where there seemed to be one clear, single, dominant cause, such as a scientist's experiments achieving no results, the analysis of what happened must consider either why the supervisor did not appreciate the problem or why the student failed to heed the supervisor's advice; and whatever answer is given raises fresh questions in need of an answer. Moreover, for most students there was no apparent single cause of failure other than the student having worked too slowly. This may be an adequate explanation in many cases, but there is a strong tautological element in it. Apart from those who gave up their researches or studies before the end of the normal period, of all these students it could be said that to have achieved a successful thesis would have involved doing more and making more rapid progress in the time available. And so, in a sense, nearly all of them failed because they did not work fast enough.

We are still left with the question of why they did not work fast enough, whether they could have been guided into more efficient and effective methods of research, whether their plans could have been changed so that they had more manageable programmes, etc. which takes us into the field of supervision, with which the next chapter is concerned.

8

Supervision

A number of the students I interviewed were warm in their praise of their supervisors. Others described their supervision more as a curate's egg – excellent in parts.

Where there was criticism of the supervisor it was often given at first with some reluctance; though sometimes (certainly not every time) a veritable flood welled out once it started. A good impression of the way these comments and criticisms arose is provided by the following extract.

> ER. He didn't call you in himself of his own accord to ask how you were getting on?
>   Yes, he did occasionally; but I don't think it was more than once a term. I'm not really trying to shuffle off blame for my not having finished onto an absent supervisor. He wasn't there, but when I've said that I regarded research as a solitary business, I do also regard it as something I have to regulate and complete, so the failure to finish lies squarely with me.

The critical comments were rather like those made by current students in my earlier survey. The difference here was that it was possible to relate specific criticisms to what had gone wrong, and it was possible for me, by taking the student through the whole story of his research or course of study, to perceive shortcomings in the supervision of which the student did not tell me – indeed could not tell me since he was unaware of them himself.

The range of comments, complaints and shortcomings revealed was substantial. At one extreme, the student was sometimes patently trying to shift onto the supervisor the blame for difficulties that were largely his own fault. At the other extreme there were cases of grave neglect and dereliction of duty. In between were many cases which could reflect the substantial differences of view held amongst university staff on the nature and scope of a supervisor's duties and on the best way of carrying them out.

The supervisor of postgraduate research is appointed for his knowledge of the student's field, or perhaps because it is his turn to be allocated one of his department's quota of studentships, or perhaps in order to even out the teaching load within the department. It is generally assumed that anyone capable of holding a lectureship is capable of supervising a research student – after all, many universities' contracts specify that their staff shall engage in research, and if one can do research, one can, presumably, supervise it. It is only recently, with the publication of the SERC's excellent booklet on supervision (Christopherson et al. 1982), that there has been any apparent recognition even of the need to offer supervisors advice on their difficult task.

There are, of course, substantial differences from field to field in the skills the supervisor needs. Also the accepted common approach to supervision in some fields would be unacceptable in others: for example, that the supervisor plays a more active part in students' research in chemistry than in other fields can be deduced from both the comments of leading chemists, who say that research students are needed to do their departments' research, and the high proportion of chemistry students' publications in which authorship is shared with the supervisor. Nevertheless, there are many features of the supervisor's task and problems they have to meet that are common to a wide range of subjects. There is little in the advice offered by the SERC working party that is not just as relevant to the historian as to the physicist.

OVERALL PLANNING

It is the view of some university teachers, especially historians, that it does not matter how long a postgraduate student spends over his research, and that in many cases the greater contribution to scholarship of those who spend longer on their research justifies the longer time. Against this I would argue (a) that the longer a student spends on his research, the greater the likelihood that he will not complete it, and will thus make no contribution to scholarship at all, (b) that it is only in the academic world, and not always even there, that the time spent on research can be extended indefinitely, so that, as a training for employment, the research completed to a timetable is the more valuable, and (c) that in most fields the leading scholars complete their research relatively quickly − indeed some of those arguing that time does not matter in their field seem themselves to publish books at enviably short intervals.

If completion within a given time is accepted as an aim − and most universities apparently do accept this since their regulations impose a maximum time within which the thesis must be completed − it follows that both the student and the supervisor must have some rudimentary timetable in their minds from the start. As the planning of the research proceeds, this timetable should become firmer. It should be agreed between the supervisor and the student that, at a certain point, he should move from spending all his time on general exploratory reading to the next stage − whether that is more focused reading, building his apparatus, designing a questionnaire, or beginning searches in record offices. They should agree at what point to start submitting written drafts, at what point experimental work, collection of material, etc. should stop, when full-time writing should begin, and so on. As work proceeds and it becomes clear that certain parts of the overall plan cannot be achieved, they should modify it.

Some may regard this as an unattainable ideal − in their field there is too great an element of the unexpected in research for such planning to be feasible. I believe, however, that one of the characteristics that divide the good from the pedestrian researcher is the ability to anticipate the unexpected. Although there are some difficulties met in research that no one can overcome, many others can be defeated or circumvented. The good researcher, though unable to foresee the precise nature of every problem that will arise, will have some idea in advance of the general nature of the obstacles that will be met, and will have various alternative plans, if not ready, at least at the back of his mind. For research that has to be completed within a given time, the obstacles that have to be overcome are not merely the things that cannot be done in a particular way — the experiments that fail, the apparatus that will not work — but also the things that cannot be done within the time available.

A proper apprenticeship in research will set the student on the road to solving or circumventing such difficulties for himself. However, he is unlikely to receive such an apprenticeship at the hands of a supervisor who either cannot himself do that or, worse still, cannot even see the need to do it.

The people I interviewed often told me of their own accord of the lack of any planning to complete their research within a time that would not too greatly exceed the three years for which they generally held studentships. Where they did not do so I asked them questions about the extent to which they had discussed the timing of their work, whether they had, at any point, worked out with their supervisor how long each stage could be expected to take and drawn up any overall plan and timetable, at what stage they started to realize that the work would not be completed within the three years, and so on.

Very few of them had at any point been told how they should phase their work to complete it in three years or discussed any timetable for their research with their supervisors — the mere idea that they might have done so came as a surprising novelty to many of them. This is probably one of the most significant differences between the less successful students I interviewed in this study and the more successful ones I have met in other contexts.

The failure to ensure that the students' research was properly planned often went, however, far beyond the lack of any kind of timetable. One student had failed his PhD at the University of B..., having been given an MSc for his thesis; he then joined the staff of a government-funded research institute attached to the University of C..., where he was registered for a PhD for which, when I saw him, he had virtually completed the work. He was thus able to contrast two approaches to research.

> I was left in the traditional B... system where they throw you in at the shallow end when you go, and they hope you'll come out of the deep end at the end of three years, and if you happen to drown in the middle, well, isn't that a pity, but there we are. It's been a great contrast coming from that sort of system, where I muddled through and made every mistake in the book, to come here which is a research institute; and here we have got people who are professional researchers, and you don't make mistakes in experimental planning; and now to do a PhD here, it's a doddle. In some ways I feel entitled to get it because I did the work somewhere else; but now if I do an experiment here it works; there's no question of it not working. You may not get the answer you want, but the answer you get is still valuable and can be written down, where at B... one often ended up with nothing.

Although most supervisors had made no attempt that registered with the student to impress on him the implications of having a finite length of time in which to complete the research, there were a few who clearly realized the need for an overall plan and were also able to get the idea through to the student. The following quotations come from a literature student and a biologist respectively.

> I did discuss overall strategy with my second supervisor, but that was modified, and my final supervisor was tending to push me for my bits of completed work and we didn't discuss any overall strategy, though obviously she was aware I was completing the time allotted. I think she was anxious at the time that I should get something done that she could read, which I did; but, of course that was very late on.

> I wouldn't want to put any sort of blame on her because I think she was really very good and sort of bustled me along. (The student then talked about the differences in techniques needed between the supervisor's field of research and his own, and continued) ... So I don't think she really had a grasp of the difficulties of this work, but she gave me every encouragement and help all the time.

A music student who saw his supervisor about once a term gave this description of the supervision:

> I did occasionally manage to put some words down which she took away and read and sent back with a few comments on the bottom. (When the student saw the supervisor) she'd say 'What do you think you're going to do next?' You'd say it and she'd say 'Have you got any problems?' and you'd attempt to formulate what you thought were the problems, and she'd suggest a few ways of treating them. They tended to be fairly general chatty sessions.
>
> ER. Did she discuss the general overall strategy, timing, how long you'd spend on each bit, and what was going to be in the work altogether?
>
> Not really. What was going to be in the work altogether, perhaps. I can't recall it, but we may have talked through the basic argument and its expansion, and such conclusions as are feasible from that, but I can't think that anything in more detail was ever talked about. I occasionally put things down on paper, planned things out for her. She'd say, 'That looks OK. Fine. When you've got something to show me show me'.

UNSTRUCTURED SUPERVISION

The students themselves were more aware of another common weakness in supervision — that the supervisor did not give it any structure, but tended to 'play it by ear', to give no advance thought or planning to his function as a supervisor but, instead, to regard it as adequate that he should be available to see the student and do his best to answer whatever questions the student might raise. There are three disadvantages to this system beyond the lack of attention to the need to complete the work within a finite time; first, if the student were floundering, or simply idle, the supervisor would not discover that unless the student chose to reveal it; secondly, the student's ability to get help depended on his knowing what questions to ask; and thirdly, even where this was not the intention, the student may have felt discouraged from taking up the supervisor's time except in great need.

As some of them put it:

> He had a fairly general knowledge of the area, well, more than a general knowledge, a detailed knowledge without it being his own particular concern of study. ... But it was all, I now see — well, I saw at the time, actually — very unstructured, and it required me to have decided what I wanted from him, to be able to pose the right questions to get the feedback right — not uncommon in the arts, but a fatal procedure if you're not absolutely sure what you're doing.

> In fact what has happened in the past year is that Professor Jones has appointed another supervisor as well and he's keeping me to a much tighter deadline to revise and produce things.

> I felt I should perhaps have tried to plan in advance more what to do, although, since I was breaking into ground that I hadn't covered at all as an undergraduate, I think this would have been very difficult; and I think this is where I could have appreciated more help from my supervisor whose general attitude was 'Come to me when you're in trouble, but otherwise you need to be left alone'. Contrasting this to the handling of other research students by their supervisors which I got to hear of, I felt that in a way I was on too loose a rein. By the time I felt I was in trouble it had gone past the point where I could go back to him and say 'Can you help sort it out?'

It may be of some interest that two of these respondents now hold posts in universities, and the other in a polytechnic. The next comment comes from an advanced course student who did not attempt a research project, but it is on the same theme of supervision being too slack.

> Perhaps if I'd been forced to read in one closely defined direction I would have achieved more in the end, though perhaps I wouldn't have enjoyed it quite so much as it was happening.

Naturally, the supervisors who did not believe in structuring their supervision saw their students to discuss their research with them relatively infrequently.

> It was a funny relationship. I accepted it then, but now it seems inconceivable that the supervisor never came to see the experiment or to see the animals, and I saw him every six months. I saw him all the time but we didn't discuss the research. And then, every six or nine months, I would cart along a heap of results and he would then say, 'Oh, very interesting', or he might say something infuriating like 'I really think you should have measured Y'. And so I would have to do the whole lot again and measure Y, which one should have thought of to start with.

I was left for six months with no direction and gradually I managed to work my way through to some things that might have been useful to do and I did a few things and plotted a few things and full of the joys of spring presented them to my supervisor, who was duly not impressed. Not that he said anything, it was just that he nodded wisely and said 'Yes. Go away and do some more'. And that was it. It continued like that for the rest of the time.

He didn't seem to enjoy supervising research students, and if you asked to see him he'd give you a date three weeks in advance. But I knew this was going to be a problem before I went there; I'd been warned so I didn't feel hard-done-by really.

Often the need to provide structured supervision slipped out of sight because the supervisor was too busy, or had forgotten how long it was since he had last had a thorough discussion with the student.

I didn't get enough supervisor contact on a sit-down-and-let's-talk-about-what-you've-done-this-week basis. We always intended to do it, but it never happened. I was not so enthusiastic because I didn't really enjoy sitting down and saying 'Well, I've got nowhere this week'; and he was far too busy to press the matter, I think, at that time. So I don't think I got as much disciplining in that sort of sense as I might have done in other circumstances.

Many of the comments that I have quoted above, or will quote below, implied some degree of neglect of his duties on the part of the supervisor. Sometimes, however, the student explicitly said something like the following extract.

ER. Were you seeing him every day?
    I was seeing him pretty well all the time.
    ER. He was working alongside you?
    That's right. It was the opposite of the usual complaint — I never see my supervisor. He was there all the time, but the interaction with him was almost never actually to do with my research work, or the research work I should have been doing. It appeared that he wasn't interested. He was supervising PhD students because that was one of the things he had to do as part of his job. In fact his other pupils, his pupils that succeeded, tended to keep themselves away from him, go and hide somewhere, and only arange to see him occasionally when they'd sort of get him in a corner and say 'Right; the following aspects of my work need discussing'; and they'd sort of work him through it.

THE CLOSENESS OF SUPERVISION
One of the major dilemmas of the supervisor is to know how much advice and help to give. If he gives too much he is virtually taking over the research and using the student as a research assistant. If he gives too little, the student wastes a lot of time floundering and making elementary discoveries by making elementary mistakes. Perhaps the ideal supervisor tells the student

very little, apart from suggesting sources of material and things to read but follows the talmudic model, asking the student the penetrating questions that enable him to see for himself what he should do and how he should go about it, answering a question with another question. I suspect, however, that this approach succeeds only when both the supervisor and the student have brilliant minds. Also there are some crafts, such as questionnaire design, which have to be shown to the student — 'You do it like this'.

Certainly, one of the chief complaints of the students was that they received too little useful help.

I did feel, perhaps wrongly, that I was very much left to flounder by myself. Whether it was because I was older and they thought, therefore, that I should know all these things, I don't know; but I felt they were saying 'There you are; you've got a two-one; you're all right; now run along and do it'. And I didn't know; I was thrashing about. And I also felt that very often the comments I received, particularly from my supervisor, were interesting but not terribly helpful, in the sense of, it was all right as a comment on what I'd done, but it still didn't give me any help on what I should do next or which direction I should go in. I got plenty of reassurance, but I felt sometimes that it was rather patronizing — 'It's all right. Don't you worry' — you know, a pat on the head — 'Go along. It's fine.' And I didn't want that. I wanted some criticism with more of an edge to it, and much more constructive help.

After the first term, apart from that report, which I had to do via him and the prof, I don't recall ever having any serious discussion of how well my research was going until the end of my third year, which seemed fine for a while; and after two years you just sort of wondered whether he bothered at all.

ER. Did he work near you?

Yes.

ER. He just didn't settle down to a serious discussion of what you were doing and how you could do it?

Yes. I don't know how you'd explain it. It seemed rather odd.

ER. You didn't try to get him to talk more to you about it? Did you leave the initiative to him?

At that stage yes. Being left on your own seems fine initially. It's a question of how long it takes you to realize you haven't got anywhere. It comes down to the whole thing about whether you regard the research as being a training or research for its own sake. But if it is training, then the training in project management, just managing yourself by trial and error, is rather inefficient, which is what I think happened.

I saw very little of her; perhaps twice a year at most.

I have said above that a number of students said that their supervisors were people who tended to get sudden enthusiasms, and lose them as quickly. Their supervision was erratic, sometimes close and sometimes virtually non-existent.

He was always interested in phases. In other words he'd have one week in term when he was terribly interested in what was going on; and then, all the rest of the time, he really wasn't terribly interested, and one plodded along on one's own, and you might get a few words out of him said terribly quickly while he rushed off to follow his latest phase. He was terribly nice but not terribly helpful in that sense at times.

When I got my grant I was supposed to be working on ... but by the time I actually arrived here my supervisor, who has a very vivid lively mind and swaps around a lot from one thing to another, decided it wouldn't be worth doing and would be too difficult.

I was expected to find my own way because my supervisor had little favourite schemes of his own which were going on and these were very well directed. Unfortunately, mine wasn't one of those.

He's a great dabbler. He's now having great fun dabbling in ... at ... Polytechnic. Thoroughly enjoying himself. But he was very much one for doing a bit here and a bit there, all over the place. Drove his students to distraction. Several asked to be transferred to another supervisor because they realized they weren't going to get anywhere.
    ER. You didn't though?
    I didn't, no. I suspect because I was enjoying what I was actually doing and perhaps wasn't too keen on what I should have been doing. ... I wasn't the only one who suffered from my supervisor's jumping about all over the place. Several of his other students didn't finish for the same reason. Those who did finish, as I say, were the ones who effectively ignored him.

Donald was often not there. He had at least a year's leave of absence, et cetera, et cetera. His interest also, to be frank, was peripheral, in a sense. He was interested in the subject if he thought he could get something out of it for the work he was doing for the various House of Commons committees. I saw him at a conference last summer when I did a paper on the research. He's suddenly become very interested again. The reason is he saw some use directly for himself. Prior to that he wasn't very interested when I wrote out a paper saying this is the suggested methodology, this is what I think we ought to do.

THE SUPERVISOR'S COMPETENCE
On the whole, students were more likely to say that their supervisors were not interested in them, or only interested intermittently, than that they were simply incompetent; but there were cases where the students said that the supervisor could not himself cope with the research that the student was trying to do.

I think possibly what I lacked was strong supervision because my supervisor, though he had a PhD, was not a particularly gifted man. I think he'd got where he'd got by hard work. He would enthuse about the development of the project and the development of the ideas without, I felt, really understanding them. So whilst his enthusiasm was flattering, deep down there really wasn't anything much there. There weren't constructive comments – you know 'Why don't you take it along this way?' ... I think one thing I missed was intelligent objective comments.

I think it's mistaken to have people supervising PhDs who haven't done them themselves.
    Why?
    Because there are certain procedures, ways of going about research, that can save you a great deal of time. Let's slightly rephrase that – if not actually done a PhD, then written some substantial work and published – somebody who's tried to get to grips with that kind of effort and to bring together and synthesize a large body of material like that. I think unless you've done that you're not competent to supervise someone else in doing it.

Some of the criticisms of supervisors indicate the wide range of qualities a good supervisor needs. A capacity for taking an interest in what the student is doing must surely be foremost amongst these.

I think the supervisor was an enormous disappointment. It wasn't that he was hostile. He filled in the forms and wrote the letters. But I never felt any interest or spark of enthusiasm. I think I could almost have managed even though he didn't know anything about the subject if he would just have sat and listened; but he made it very clear that he hadn't got time for it.

The problem arising when the supervisor knows little about the students' research topic is a difficult one. If the student is doing totally new and original work, it follows that the supervisor will not know all about it. But he does need to know about closely related fields, and especially fields using the same methodology. And he must have sufficient experience and knowledge of, and feeling for, the processes and procedures of research to understand what the student is trying to do and to nudge him in the right direction. Moreover, he must have a clear notion of how to supervise a student in a topic that is not entirely in his own field, and must not be tempted to push the student into his own immediate area of research.

I suppose one problem was that his interests were not the same as mine proved to be, and he was therefore constantly trying to edge me into areas that he felt interested in, purely because he knew more about them and was able to offer specific guidance in that area.

It seemed to me quite often that failure to terminate certain students' studies at an early stage showed a combination of optimism, *laissez-faire* and blindness that amounted to negligence. Some students took the same view.

Having said that I was a difficult person to talk to, I think the people who were around me shouldn't have been so reserved. I mean, they were very reserved. I think anybody with any common-sense would have realized I wasn't getting on with it and wasn't very happy, and I think it probably would have taken somebody getting angry with me. Maybe that's a difficult thing to ask, but I don't think so. I don't know if it would have been different in any other discipline. I think they looked on themselves as rather tolerant and easy-going, and they wouldn't have wanted to see themselves as a kind of harsh parent; but in some cases I think a harsh parent is required.

THE SUPERVISOR'S ABSENCE OR DEPARTURE

One quite predictable problem that turned up from time to time was that the supervisor had gone away, at least temporarily. Given that studentships last three years, but that the student often continues his research for at least a year or two after that, and also given that staff can in many universities take paid study leave for one year in seven, one could expect the supervisors of more than half the students to be away at some point in their research. If one then takes into account unpaid leave of absence the odds increase, even before any account is taken of the possibility that a member of staff might be within five years of retirement when the student starts his research, or that a supervisor might gain promotion by taking a post elsewhere, or change jobs for other reasons.

The following case is better than many. Often, if his supervisor is away and no substitute supervisor has been appointed, the student has hardly any help from anyone else — the supervisor is likely to be the only expert on the student's subject in the department. (In this case, the student had a research studentship for only a little over two years as he had previously attended a postgraduate course.)

I had my supervisor for one year in total. For the other year and three months he was off in Australia.

ER. Did you have anybody else taking his place?

Not formally. There were of course the other people — other lecturers, professors in the department — who I had contact with from time to time and who I went to with specific problems; but there was no-one giving general direction to my work. That's one part where I think things would certainly have been different if I'd have had a supervisor there all the time, because I think that would have encouraged me to have got more done whilst I was there. I think, without the supervision, I fell into the trap of carrying on working not realizing how hard it would be to write up the thesis. I then started the thesis far too late.

Perhaps the easiest problem to deal with is this simple failure to appoint a substitute supervisor during the main supervisor's absence. It seems to me an astonishing dereliction of duty, very revealing of the attitudes towards the whole task of supervision that are occasionally to be found. The other problems that arose from these absences and departures were of a number of kinds.

A student did not get on with the new supervisor, who wanted to impose a different style of work on him. Although the supervisor may well have been right in regarding the student's established approach as unsatisfactory, it was by then too late to impose a radical change. The first supervisor, as often happens, did not return from his sabbatical, and relations between the student and his new supervisor seem simply to have broken down, with the new supervisor failing to return drafts that were sent him.

In another case a member of staff who, though not formally the student's supervisor, was the leading figure in the team of which he was part, went to a chair elsewhere, taking with him a highly innovative piece of apparatus he had built that was crucial to the team's work. He left behind a prototype, which could not always be induced to work.

When a department has an appointed head (as distinct from one elected for a set period), there are problems in his last years before he retires, and fresh problems later while his successor tries out new ideas and finds his way. I interviewed two students from the same major department who had been on opposite sides of a divide of this kind. Here is the first student's account of it:

> I think the professor knew there were problems. However, he was on the point of retiring. He had lots of other interests apart from his ... group. By that stage one year he was President of the Institute of Chemical Engineers and he sat on various committees so he was very much an absent professor so he didn't actually take much notice of the running of his group.

The second student said:

> At this point in time − horrible phrase − there was a new professor of chemical engineering appointed, and he was from (a multinational firm) where they'd obviously got all the facilities laid on, and he sort of took over this project. So he was probably in equal ignorance to me as to the actual facilities that were available within the university.

He then described in some detail the results of the consequent miscalculation of what a student could do without the kind of assistance and equipment available to researchers in industry.

Another student described what happened after his supervisor went to America and decided to stay there, while the student himself had taken a fairly responsible research post in a university other than that at which he was registered for his PhD, on which he had then done two years' work. It is worth quoting his account at some length because it illustrates some of the complexities of these individual cases.

> After I came to E... I saw him about four times in two years and I used to send him work as well, but it was a fairly unsatisfactory relationship, and I think one of the principle reasons why I didn't finish my thesis was because of that supervision relationship. Would you like me to give you an example about one particular thing? The statistical work that I was doing on ...; about two months after I got to E... I actually produced a write-up of that work and sent it off. He sent it back with a few criticisms and things, and then, about six months later, I saw him and he said 'Well, this statistical work is really not good enough. You really ought to be analysing it much deeper. You ought to be collecting some more facts and some more figures'. And that meant that the one chapter which I thought

I'd more or less finished actually turned into something that I had to do a lot more work on. And although when I went to E... the agreement was that I'd have time to work on the thesis, for various reasons the time I had was very limited and I just couldn't get on with the work fast enough.

ER. Had he known what data you were collecting beforehand?

Yes, he knew what data I was collecting.

ER. So that he too had made a mistake if you needed other data?

I think that's true. I think one of the problems was that I was quite a headstrong person the two years that I was a postgraduate at D..., and I'd very much decided before I became a postgraduate student exactly what it was I wanted to do, and I went off and did that. And I think one of the problems was that Robert himself was having all kinds of personal and academic problems and there just wasn't a close enough relationship between us in terms of frequency and continuity of supervision for it to really work.

Among the many strands in this account, the one that is of most significance here is the time-lag in communication between the supervisor and the student. It is natural that a supervisor should have second (and sometimes third) thoughts about his student's research. After he has made some general comments on a piece of work and handed it back he may realize that it has some more serious shortcomings. But if he is not working in the same place as the student he is less likely to pass on his further comments and criticisms immediately.

Two students reported their work being seriously affected by their supervisors dying.

RELATIONS WITH SUPERVISOR, OTHER STAFF, AND FELLOW STUDENTS

A number of students said that they just could not get on with their supervisors. A few such clashes of personality are inevitable, and they usually cannot be regarded as anybody's fault. However, in one case a student reported that she could not get on with a supervisor who expected her to produce work at regular intervals – she could not produce work that frequently – so was changed to another, much less demanding, supervisor, with whom she also could not get on. She had also mentioned various other dislikes for other people, and certain specific psychological problems she had had, so it was easy to guess where the difficulty lay.

The reasons mentioned for liking or disliking a supervisor were, as one would expect, very varied. Some disliked the erection of a social barrier by the supervisor, but some preferred it. On the whole students seemed to feel more at ease with supervisors who went out of their way to maintain a friendly relationship. One student who said he always felt uneasy in the presence of his supervisor (someone I knew, about whom I felt the same) also said there was nothing on which he could place his finger to account for this, except for one detail:

He was working on some of the same poets that I was working with, and there were one or two occasions when I came up with something I'd read which he hadn't read and he said 'Oh yes; that's interesting' and out came the notebook, which of course is the classic thing about supervisors — very off-putting for the researcher.

I usually asked the students who reported these clashes of personality with their supervisors if they had tried to discuss their research problems with other members of staff; but I was almost always told that that was regarded as unethical — any approach to other staff about their research should be made through their supervisors. I was told more than once that to go to see someone else because they could not get on with their supervisors would be rather like making a public announcement that a marriage is breaking down, damaging to both sides.

One student who was in a big, and prestigious, department said that there was a graduate student counsellor in the department, but when he tried to see him he found he was away on sabbatical.

A more common response to this kind of problem is to turn to fellow students, especially those a year or two ahead. A number of students mentioned getting help from such sources, and fellow students seem to be especially helpful in providing guidance over the more elementary problems of research — the kind of problem which the supervisor would not even think to discuss and which the student would feel was too trivial to raise with him. I was less sure that fellow students would be a good source of guidance through more complicated and fundamental problems. It seemed to me that more often the blind would be leading the blind — though that is also, on occasions, a fair description of help from the appointed supervisor.

As occasional clashes of personality between students and supervisors are inevitable, one would expect departments to provide some means of detecting and dealing with these. However, my interviews strongly suggested that in many departments such mechanisms were either missing or were not fully effective.

NEGLECT

One of the most striking forms of supervisor's neglect I met was the retention of students' drafts for an inordinately long time. Not all the complaints of this kind seemed wholly justified. To keep the eighth draft of a chapter three weeks seems to me execusable — the supervisor might well have been having understandable difficulty in bringing himself to read it yet once more or pondering what there was new he could say about it. But three students mentioned that their drafts had been with their supervisors for over a year. It is possible in these cases that the supervisor could not bring himself to tell the student how terrible the work was — though this seems to be an utterly inadequate excuse. It certainly could not be the explanation in another case known to me where the student gained a PhD in well below the median time for the subject and where most of the lateness (beyond three years) in presentation of the thesis was due to the supervisor spending over six months reading the draft. The student made appointments to see him which he simply failed to keep.

Often a student whose supervisor is holding a draft for so long can, in the meantime, do no further work, and it is difficult to regain the lost impetus.

One of the questions that interested me here is why, when a student is not getting effective supervision and useful advice, or the supervisor does not turn up for an appointment, or the supervisor is simply not reading the drafts, the student does nothing about it. The answer varies according to the individual circumstances — the particular problem or form of neglect. Sometimes, as in problems that arise from inadequate or bad advice on the choice of a topic, or the lack of adequate help with the planning, or lack of initial instruction in relevant techniques, the student is not aware of the problem at all, or becomes aware of it too late to do anything effective about it. Sometimes there is no obvious person to whom a complaint can be made. Sometimes the student feels that a complaint will do more harm than good — the staff can be expected to close ranks against the complainant. Quite often the student feels, perhaps rightly, that he has been in some way to blame himself, and does not want to draw attention to this. Very often, the explanation is that the supervisor is the only expert in the student's field of study in the particular university, so there is no real alternative. Sometimes, as I have said, there is a feeling that the problem is a private one between the student and the supervisor, and that, as with the problems in a marriage, it ought to be sorted out in private — making it public would cause a resentment that would make it worse. Moreover — and this is very important — the student is going to need good references from the supervisor when looking for a job, and possibly even when changing jobs, for some years to come.

It is worth quoting at length the comment of a student who at the time of the interview was awaiting the *viva voce* examination on a completed PhD thesis.

> I found it very difficult because my supervisor would look at work — well, to begin with he didn't even look at work. He was having problems of his own, but, nonetheless, if you take someone on you have got some responsibilities towards them. All the time there was one individual who was my undergraduate supervisor who was reading stuff and who was saying 'I'm not really competent to comment on this but ...'. So then I thought I've got to precipitate something, so, just about the time when I went off and got this job I said, 'I'm going to submit. I've finished'. So then at last he sat down and read it and said, 'Well, x, x and x is wrong', and it was very annoying because my supervisor, when he does pull the stops out is extremely good. I don't feel I ought to comment on how good he is, really is. But there's a sense in which he's a lousy teacher and will never be any good as a teacher, as people who are very good often are — lousy teachers that is. I think one needs protecting from that. He muddled me horribly. When he eventually did begin to comment we were at cross purposes. This may be an individual thing, but there are other students I've spoken to and they do know what I mean. The same has applied to all his PhD students; it's been the same for all of us. We've just been thoroughly bewildered. It's taken all of us the maximum number of extensions and God knows what to finish. That's partly why I talk about there's a need for some sort of structure, because I think if there is an individual like that there should be some kind of safety net to help protect his students. So eventually I produced drafts, and after various bust-ups we got onto a rather better footing and began to get a little bit of the kind of supervision that I needed. But I feel very ambivalent about the sort of supervision that I've had because I think there's a sense in which it's been

catastrophic. I would hate to try and blame someone else for things, and I realize there are other things I could have done. But if you add together all the various stresses that there are on a graduate student, to expect them to manage in the face of certain aspects of appalling supervision, which I think often is the case, from talking to other graduate students, I think it can be made very much more tough than it need be if that happens.

The reference to the supervisor having personal (generally marital) problems that might explain the student being neglected, drafts not being read, etc. is something that constantly recurs in the interviews.

THE QUALITY OF COURSES

In past interviews with current students I have found a substantial level of dissatisfaction with the quality of certain taught courses. I interviewed too few taught course students in this study for such discontent to appear on a significant scale, but one comment is nevertheless worth quoting.

I found that the teaching at... on the course I attended was not as well organized as I had known many years before as a younger man at .... I don't mean to be patronizing when I say this or anything like that, but I found that a new breed of don had emerged – young men and women in their twenties or early thirties – who seemed to me rather more like the up-and-coming sixth form master of one's grammar school days than a university don. It's quite unreal to have these pictures based on experience of years before, but that's how I reacted; and so having to attend seminars conducted by dons, young or middle-aged, who didn't seem to have their work prepared, who'd come in of an evening – seminars were usually in the evening – and say 'Now, what shall we do this evening', in other words, 'I haven't really prepared anything, but you can bring up something if you like, and we can discuss it'. That seemed to me disappointing, and also the level of commitment to the actual subject and the level of seriousness at which discussions were pitched seemed to me disappointing. One was offered, for example, texts to read by beat poets like Alan Ginsberg, or novelists like Norman Mailer who, interesting writers though they are, in the total perspective of American literature, didn't seem to me, and still don't seem to me, to have the level of seriousness of Herman Melville or Nathaniel Hawthorne or of Mark Twain and people of that sort. So I thought there was a certain trivial level of discussion implicit in the choice of authors.

Later in the interview he went on to say that most of the students on the course, who were mainly mature students, felt as he did about the superficiality of the teaching, and that he was astonished to find that amongst the staff running it only one, older than the rest, had published anything.

STUDENTS' VIEWS ON HOW SUPERVISION SHOULD BE DONE

Many students spoke of how they thought their research or other postgraduate studies should have been organized and supervised. Some-times I asked a question on this; sometimes the comments arose spontaneously. Some, for example, suggested that the summer vacation between graduating and the start of postgraduate study should be used for preparatory courses. Another, following the same theme, said:

> I think people ought to be trained, brought much more to a gradual change. I think this being left to sink or swim works very well for some people, but for a lot of people it just makes life unnecessarily hard. It's a waste of their time. I don't think you necessarily learn to be a better research historian through having done it all for yourself from the very beginning. I also think there's a need for a briefing of research students. I realized, I think, part way through, or quite early on, that I did not have a sufficient command of one or two skills to do the job properly, which I ought to have had when I started and which I had to waste time acquiring. Particularly my knowledge of Latin was not good enough to start with, and that was always a problem.... There is a need for a more rigorous briefing in the skills you are going to need – do you have them? If not, what are you going to do about getting them? ... Firms come round saying 'This is what we want, this is what we are looking for; are you interested?', and list the job. The same sort of thing ought to be done at research level – if you're going to be doing research in ... these are the sort of things you ought to be considering – and how you are going to make sure you're going to match your ability and your particular skills and particular interests you're doing, and how to set about working it out. I'm sure that could be done quite easily. I'm sure many people do it for themselves.

A number of the respondents touched in one way or another on this general theme that the student should not be left to sink or swim.

I have quoted above from a student who contrasted the professionalism with which research was carried out in a research institute with the amateur approach to research of the university department in which he had earlier been working for a PhD. Another compared the supervision he had received in his home university with a period spent in America.

> I feel that Peter did not have enough grip on either me or on the subject. I wish he'd been more disciplinarian about it. I wish he didn't just read through what I'd written, make a few off comments and say 'Well, see you next month and bring me what you've done then'. That I didn't need. In America I had something quite different. My professor there was very dynamic, and if I'd stayed in America I think I would have finished it by now; because she was very precise as to exactly what she'd have wanted if the PhD had been for her institution, and it was almost like writing an essay each week. That would have been a chapter, and that would have been a chapter. It was all very clear cut.

A typical example of another approach to the sink-or-swim theme is well represented by the following quotation:

> Becoming a postgraduate, I think, except for a very, very few people whose whole life is their work, is a very traumatic experience after being an undergraduate; and I think a lot of departments don't make an effort to integrate postgraduates into the life of the department, socially and

intellectually. And I think one thing a postgraduate wants above all is to talk to other people about their subject; and probably one thing they need is to talk to other people about things other than their subject but still in the discipline. In other words, the broader education should be continued, and this is something we've been very hot on at T... (the university at which he teaches).

The following comments come in turn from students in technology, experimental science, social studies and the arts, but there is virtually nothing in them specific to any one field. Three of the four taught in a university or polytechnic.

I think really all it needs is somebody who will say 'Right, what have you done in the last month?' and make you explain it to yourself as well as to somebody else. It's just a question of a regular review of what you're doing so that you can pick up the fact that it's six months — it didn't seem that long but in fact it is that long — since the last noticeable piece of progress happened.

I said to myself when I get to supervise people there are things that I'm going to drum into their heads and make it absolutely clear — this is a three-year shot; you start here and you come out of here in three years with a degree.

I think it taught me how not to do it. I think the most obvious thing is that you need to be given rather more time than more people seem to be willing to. I think it also suggests to me that if you're supervising somebody you've got to be rather harder than anybody in S... ever was with me — and not only me but other people there as well. I think you've got, once you start to talk to the character, to make them have a far more rigid programme — not rigid in the sense that it's got to be totally kept to and so forth — I think more rigid than I've got.

ER. More thought out perhaps?

Not from the very beginning. One of the distinctions between a social science and natural science is the extent to which the topic is your own and you have to think about it and think of the methodology, and I think that's important. I think the doing of the research, writing the programs, is useful, but intellectually, thinking out the project, the programme proper, yourself, is important — I think I learnt more from that.... I think you've got to allow the student to actually think out his own topic, to write it down, but then to be willing to comment on it fairly rigorously — 'I think this is too ambitious; it's not on' or 'Miss out X, Y and Z'. Then, having got that far, you've got to actually set deadlines for producing things — 'How about doing a literature review of topic X, Y, Z, whatever, by so and so?'. Then you've got to write comments on it. At S... I was left far too much trying to discipline myself. There was literally no work discipline, which in almost everything else you do you've at least got — if it's only to give lectures and so forth. Also I think you've got to be interested in the subject, and I think too many postgrads get taken on to places where the staff are not really not very interested.

It's very easy to assume that people know what they're doing and I think you have to find tactful ways of providing the kind of close supervision that you would give an undergraduate for a longer stage than is generally accepted as necessary in the arts; and that, depending on what the topic is, it may be that, not exactly new methods of research have to be evolved, but only a framework has to be evolved. My subject, for instance, is still a very untried field, the bibliography is by no means controlled. You may well have to do a lot of that basic work yourself with the student to begin with, to make sure they really are doing something. And the other thing, I think, is just damn well keep in touch with your student. Don't assume if they're away for six weeks from you that they haven't been trying to contact you, and might need you, but set up a pattern of regular meetings and of regular monitoring.

GROUP RESEARCH

In an increasing number of fields today major research has to be done by groups of research workers rather than by the lone individual. This is now true of nearly all of science and technology, and of large parts of the social sciences. Even in the humanities, especially in those fields such as social history and linguistics which border on the social sciences, some research is being done by groups. Therefore, if the purpose of studying for a research degree is an apprenticeship leading to a career in research, it makes sense, in many cases, to train the student in group rather than solo research.

This is the main argument for involving research students in group research; but it also seems an attractive solution to some of the problems of the supervision of students that I have reported above. The theory is that the student in a research group gets help and advice from all the more senior members of the research team − both teaching staff and research fellows, etc. − one of whom acts as his supervisor, keeping a more systematic watch on his progress. Also the students have more regular and focused discussions of their work with each other. If for any reason there is a need for a change of supervisor, there are other members of staff who already know the student, are working in the same field, and are ready to take over.

That is the theory. The practice is a little different, and it is worth looking at the cases that actually came my way. Of course it is possible that these are unrepresentative, that the supervision of research students within group research is so successful that the students from research groups would be extremely unlikely to come into the population from which my sample was drawn. It is possible, but I do not for one moment belive it, and neither would anyone else looking at this with an open mind.

The students whose cases I describe below are not the only ones who were working in what their supervisors or departments might well describe as a research group. Indeed, all the students in science and technology could have been so described; but this would in general only mean that the supervisor or department had more than one student doing research in a similar area, not that they were in any sense co-operating on joint research. These students have been selected for discussion because they were either engaged in joint research or part of something that had the formal title of a research group. The problems they described are various.

These are the problems.

One result of the increasing importance that has been attached to group research in recent years has been a tendency to label all the research done in related fields within the same department as group research, regardless of whether there is any closer connection between the researchers than is normally found between two people working in the same department. This is the explanation for the astonishingly high proportion of students — ranging between subjects from 71 per cent to 97 per cent — who were reported to be engaged in group research by the regrettably naive survey carried out for the Swinnerton-Dyer Working Party by the Policy Studies Institute (Whalley 1982). Although universities are dedicated to the pursuit of truth, where money or their other major interests are concerned, anything they say needs no less rigorous a scrutiny than that which the Inland Revenue give to tax claims. (For a minor example of this see Rudd, 1980.)

One example of this re-labelling came my way. I interviewed six students who had worked for PhDs in the same department — one whose status as a major research and teaching department in science and technology is beyond dispute. Four of them had first class honours degrees, one being the best first of his year from a large department to which entry is highly competitive. Four were working in the same general area, and seem to have been members of a part of the department that had given itself the title of a research group and a name suggesting that it was engaged in technological research of vital significance to industrial progress in an area where Britain is lagging behind her competitors; however, I did not actually ask each student if he was a member of this group as I was not at first aware of its existence and its significance for my study. Also one other student, of whom I shall say more below, said he was a member of it.

There was no possibility of collusion between the students I saw, but there was no conflict in the stories they told me, and the same points tended to be repeated — for example that the Science Research Council (as it then was) had pumped large sums into the group in the form of research grants and studentships, but the group was so bad at supervising students, and had so little idea about the research the students could do, that few of them were gaining their doctorates; and that the group was not interested in practical applications of the theory it was developing, regarding any practical use of its theory as years into the future — an unsatisfactory state of affairs for a student who believes he has come to do applicable research. Several of them gave me figures for the numbers of their contemporaries setting out to gain PhDs and the numbers succeeding.

The account they gave me of their research and their relations with other staff strongly indicated that it was, at best, a loosely organized group within which their research differed in only one respect from the solo and individual research done by students in, say, a modern-language department. The difference was that each supervisor had far more students, so there was more opportunity for informal interaction, though this seems to have taken place only at a superficial level. Those who reported difficulties with their supervisors all said that they could not have taken their problems to other members of staff.

One student had wandered off to do research in the social sciences, in a field remote from any in which either he or his supervisor had any competence. I do not know whether his registration for research within the department and his studentship should simply have been terminated, or whether he should have been transferred to another department and to support by the SSRC, but that he was allowed to continue as he did was little short of a scandal.

It was clear from conversation with the university's graduate office, before the interviews, that they were well aware there was something amiss in that department, though they probably did not know what it was. There is no way in which a research council can police that kind of situation, though they might perhaps be more circumspect about the way in which they try to promote particular activities with generous offers of money.

A second major problem is illustrated by two students who were working for PhDs in the kind of university research groups that would seem to the outsider to be ideal for the training of research students; these were tightly organized groups run by a highly productive researcher. Both students had firsts, one being the top first of his year in a major department. In both cases there were probably contributory causes for their failure to complete, but the team research was in large measure responsible for their not completing on time, and so for substantially reducing the probability of their completing at all.

Selection of a topic for a PhD is never easy; for example, it must be neither too large nor too small, it must have adequate theoretical elements, etc. Where the group's research takes the form of a series of experiments — for example, work on large machines in particle physics — the selection of a topic is not too difficult, as the student can be given an experiment, or a series of experiments to design and write up. Where, however, the group's research is essentially a single entity, aimed at the solution of a major problem, it is sometimes difficult to find a thesis-sized piece of research that can easily be hived off for the student to do. In one of these cases, the student spent eighteen months assembling pieces of work that might form a connected whole (ie he was half-way through his studentship) before it was decided what his topic would be.

Another problem arises when the student is asked to take on minor problems not relevant to his thesis research. This can be excellent training — indeed, ideally, the student should have a go at as many different parts of the team's work as possible — but it does get in the way of completing, and even more of writing up as a thesis, the student's research on his PhD topic, especially when, as so often happens, the minor problem proves bigger than expected. Similar difficulties arise where the student has done enough work for his thesis but is expected to carry his work further to produce the results, gadgetry, or whatever, that others need. One said: 'I think there was bias towards getting it working rather than getting our theses written.' This is understandable. Getting it working is the main aim of the enterprise and is bound to seem more important than an individual's PhD if there is a major clash. The problem, however, is not what happens in a major clash of interest, but what happens in a series of minor clashes, and the tendency of the main researcher to be unaware of the impact on the student's PhD of a series of decisions each of which is of small importance in itself.

Part of the answer certainly lies in the leaders of such groups paying more attention to the needs of their PhD students; but I suspect that the main answer lies in some form of modification of the universities' expectations of what a PhD thesis should look like, to enable students who have been working in a group to present their work more easily for examination. I shall have more to say about this in Chapter 11.

Another problem was reported by one of these students. Within any kind of group, clashes of personality and similar strains are bound to arise, and it is not unknown for such strains to break the group up completely. The ordinary employee who finds his colleagues unbearable can get out and go elsewhere; but for the PhD student to do this means sacrificing the PhD. Furthermore, he is attached, for some three years, to a group that is already established and may well, at first, feel an outsider. One of them said: 'As with any group of people working together, there were not power blocks but that sort of thing. There were natural groupings, and I didn't fit into one of the natural groupings that included my supervisor.'

This is an extra risk in attaching research students to research groups, additional to the normal risk that the student will not get on with his supervisor. Good and perceptive management of the group from the top can avoid the problem, but the leader of a group of this kind is there because of his high ability at the research, which is not necessarily linked to ability at personnel management; and anyhow, he has a lot on his mind.

A third major problem is raised by a student with a first class honours degree from a department of high international status who was making an empirical study within the social sciences, and, at the end of his second year, was invited to join a research group at another university, working in the same field, which was under the joint direction of two very able professors and housed within a major institution for research in the social sciences. The major overlap between his thesis topic and the work of the research group should have enabled him to complete his thesis while working in this group. There were a number of reasons why he failed to do so, giving up after six years; but the main one seems to have been that neither of the two researchers was able to spare much time for the project, leaving virtually the whole of the direction and execution of the work to the junior staff. Also, he was unable to establish any intellectual links within the research institute.

> It was not the kind of close intellectual atmosphere that I'd had at D.... It was very distant. It was an atmosphere where people got on with their own work in their own little rooms and it wasn't really thought to be good form to talk to each other about the work you were doing.

My own impression of the institute at which he worked is that it is not as he described it; but it may well make no attempt to integrate new members of staff into the institution, or may even freeze them out — a similar problem to that of students joining an established research group which I discussed above.

The moral here, if there is one, is that it is not enough to set up an institutional framework that seems ideally suited to team research. What the people actually do within the framework is even more important.

Fourthly, there are special problems where a group engaged in inter-disciplinary research recruits a new graduate who is the sole representative of his own specialty within the team. While he may benefit from exposure to the ideas and research techniques of other disciplines, there is no one within the group with whom he can continually discuss what he is doing from the standpoint of his own subject, or from whom he can learn the research techniques of his own field. This was once my own problem as the first economist employed by the Road Research Laboratory. Someone in a similar position (a social scientist in a technological research group) whom I interviewed said she did not find this lack of guidance from anyone in her own field a problem; but she may simply have been unaware of it as she also said that one of the reasons she gave up was that the work she was trying to do was beyond her knowledge and capabilities.

A major cause of the work not being completed was a decision made by the head of the group which determined the form in which data would be collected, resulting in the time needed to analyse it being so extended that the work could not be finished. This decision was made before she arrived, against the advice of a key member of the team. But it is doubtful if she would have challenged it if she had been there. She said she tried to keep out of the way of the head of the group as much as possible as she did not get on well with him. The point here is not merely that there may be clashes of personality that foul up the work, but that also, even without these, few new graduates will want to argue strongly with an eminent head of a research group about the way the research is done. The control of the research by an experienced researcher stops the research failing as long as his decisions are right; but they can be wrong.

A fifth problem in group research impeded seven students who had been working, or were currently working, in separate research institutes, some of which were attached to a university. Two of these gave up their research during their first year, and there was little in their decision that was in any way related to the work having been done in a research institute. One came into my sample through having failed a PhD elsewhere. The remaining four all worked in government laboratories and are interesting both because they represent a form of study for a research degree that has been encouraged in recent years – dual supervision from both a university department and an outside research laboratory where the student works – and because they represent extreme cases of how that kind of arrangement can work.

One case was rather like that which I described above as my fourth example, except that here the researcher who lacked internal guidance in his own discipline had gone to a university some thirty miles away in search of it. He said he had had very useful help, and thought the lack of any visit to his laboratory by his supervisor unimportant. There were a number of reasons for the delay in his completing his thesis, which he expected to submit before long, of which one was significant for anyone doing research under similar circumstances. The researcher in a laboratory outside a university is likely to have access to more assistance – with computing, statistics, the building of equipment, etc. – than would be available in a university, and so can do more ambitious research; but if one of the key people on whom he depends then leaves, he is correspondingly more vulnerable.

The remaining three were registered for PhDs with a university which was giving them very little help – but in any case they seemed to need little help as they were getting better supervision, training and other assistance in their own laboratory than they would have done in a university. One of them was about to discuss his draft thesis with his university supervisor; but that seemed to be virtually the sum total of the work done by the university to merit the fee charged. Otherwise it was acting only as an examining body.

The difficulties they reported were of two kinds. One was again the problem of writing a thesis incorporating work which had mainly been done jointly with others. The other was the problem of finding spare time in which to write a thesis while spending the day in a demanding job — the same problem that faces the internal student who does not complete his writing-up within the currency of his studentship.

9

Had They Gained Anything?

Many of the students said at some point in the interview that they felt very guilty at giving up when so much had been done for them, or when someone else could have had their place if they had never started. And I explicitly asked most of them what they thought they had got out of their period of study – though, as with all my questions, I asked this only where it seemed appropriate, omitting, for example, to ask it of those who gave up their studies very early. Some immediately showed how far they had at least assimilated the academic approach by entering the reservation that they could not tell how far the changes in them that had taken place while they were students had resulted from their studies, how far these changes would have taken place in any case, or what they might have got out of any alternative course of action. This is, indeed the key issue. Greater maturity could be expected to come, not simply from the passage of time, but from what these students did with their time.

Moreover, here, as everywhere, we need to look at what the students said with a modicum of scepticism; for example, in the course of an interview with a student who seemed confused in virtually everything he said and in his answers to all the questions I put to him, I was told that what he had gained from his studies was that he was less confused about issues.

Only a few said they had gained nothing at all – 'The only thing I got out of it is a lot of heartache'. Most had, at least, in various ways, had a great deal of enjoyment from their period as graduate students. After I had heard a long account of all the things that went wrong for one student – a topic that was too big for him, intractible material, a change of supervisors half-way, etc., etc., culminating in his wife leaving him – as we crossed the road to the pub at the end of the interview, he said: 'Don't get me wrong. I look back on it as a golden age'.

FRIENDSHIPS AND OTHER INCIDENTAL FEATURES OF STUDENT LIFE

Nearly all those I interviewed had enjoyed their time as postgraduate students – 'I enjoyed it all a lot; it's the after-effects I haven't enjoyed so much.' For many, however, the pleasures that they regarded as their only gains came from the incidental features of being a student, such as living in a university town, or living amongst congenial people with whom they formed lasting friendships.

There's nothing I could say 'I owe that to Oxbridge' except that it's an absolutely beautiful place. Aside from the work, which I hated, I adored being in Oxbridge. It didn't matter whether or not I was part of the university, except that it meant I could get punts when nobody else could get them, and that kind of thing.

Certainly the friends I retained from D... are the friends I made during that period, not the friends I made during the period of my undergraduate time.

There have been all sorts of benefits that have spun off; well a whole variety of people that I've met and have become life-long friends — all sorts of different people in the field.

Some of them had gained their jobs through their networks of friends, and others mentioned other ways in which the friendships they had formed as postgraduate students had proved useful.

Every so often I get a call from somebody who says 'We're now working for so and so. We hear you are in a small computer firm. We have a problem. Can you solve it.' It's nice they remember me — I feel I made some impression on the other people. So it's proved useful — contacts all over the place.

ENJOYMENT OF RESEARCH
What the students most commonly said they had got from their research was the enjoyment of doing it, or of doing some part of it, such as wide reading.

The whole business of actually going and working through documents and going to the major libraries and so on I think I found pleasant in itself regardless of the eventual outcome. Perhaps if I had regarded it as a dreary but necessary task I might have been more business-like about adjusting myself towards achieving results no matter what.

I can't think of any more pleasurable things than simply sitting down in the Public Records Office with a stack of documents that I know are likely to be productive and just reading them; that I find enormously stimulating. Or discussing it with people — a rather lower order of enjoyment I think.

I immensely enjoy intellectual argument at a face-to-face level. I think the actual personal interaction of it is what is most exciting to me.

I like to do research. I like to solve problems. I like to discuss these types of things with like-minded people. Basically I enjoyed the academic atmosphere. If I had unlimited funds I would probably do something like that for ever.

The enjoyment of doing it, in the same way that one might get enjoyment from playing a violin, or playing a piano, or running a good hundred yards.

I had quite a pleasant time being in the village, doing that kind of research. I made a lot of good friends. (Anthropologist)

It gave me time to do a lot of reading, a lot of thinking I'd never have done otherwise.

I enjoyed very much the absorption of knowledge that I was undergoing in that autumn, winter and summer. I enjoyed the fact that I was setting myself a challenge and trying to answer it by reading as much as I could.

I remember being pleased that, quite by chance, I came upon an autographed manuscript of the playwright I was studying, through random searching of catalogues in the university library, and I was able to put somebody in France who was working on an edition of the man onto this, because he thought it didn't exist; so that was a pleasing moment.

In doing that kind of work, apart from the very tedious part of the job, there are times when one is drawing a mass of information together and drawing at least tentative conclusions, or perhaps discovering new problems one hadn't realized before, or rephrasing problems, or whatever, and actually coming up with ideas which, as far as one knew, were slightly different from ideas people had come up with before in relation to that material, particularly, I suppose, broader things, particularly ideas about the structure of the novel. I found that periodically to be very, very exciting. Whether it completely compensated for the rest, I'm not sure, but certainly I found that exciting.

I can remember feelings of satisfaction when I gave a half hour seminar to the department and it went off successfully; and that was talking about what I had been doing and so on. I felt that made things more worthwhile because one was able to put together a talk which made scientific sense and show slides and show there were some results. I can remember being disappointed when the time ran out because I had a bit more to fit in than I was allowed to do, and tea couldn't wait, could it?

KNOWLEDGE AND SKILLS

A number of students mentioned specific skills which they had gained during their postgraduate studies. In particular, a number said that they had learnt computing and for many this led to a change of field and a satisfying job. That few research students mentioned that they had learnt to do research may have been because they thought this was so obvious that it did not need to be mentioned. Those who did mention it, mainly did so in somewhat equivocal terms.

Where Roger did give me some guidance was into the preliminary preparatory reading I should do before designing my research; and I did a lot of that reading, so, basically, gave myself an education in that particular field. I think I now know quite a lot about doing research – since I have been here (ie in a subsequent job), I have carried out and completed two small research projects relatively quickly and efficiently. I think I learnt quite a lot about doing research through the failures (ie when a student) but I learnt all that the hard way.

A very slow and inefficiently gained idea about how to set about doing research; a certain amount of basic little skills; not really any high level technical knowledge.

I accumulated a lot of what you could call factual material, because I'd read a lot and looked at a lot of music and learnt a lot − through my Grove work, admittedly, nothing to do with my research work. I learnt a lot about research method, especially in this very curious area I study, of which I probably now have a knowledge, well, as good as anybody in this country, but self-taught, though I've been taught other things. I've become particularly interested in early music, and from that have applied techniques I learnt in study there to a later period and got much out of it.

One did indeed say:

I feel that I got a damn good training for my three years, my only regret is that all I have to show for that is an explanation that I did three years' research. There's no letters after my name, there's no piece of paper that I can wave at people and say 'Look, I worked hard. Perhaps I didn't do things in the right order, but I produced something that was worthwhile'.

Such comments were indeed rare.

Only a few students spoke of the deeper understanding of their subjects that they gained as postgraduate students. One said, for example, that he had consolidated his knowledge of statistics, another that he had a firmer understanding of history, and another that he gained a greater awareness of theological questions. This deeper understanding of their subjects is probably something that most would not think to mention, taking it for granted.

The type of history I teach in an 11 to 16 comprehensive school is very simple compared to the sort of things I was doing at W.... However, the three years I spent there did give me a confidence in handling history, and, I think, a sure footing when I was trying to experiment and when I was trying to produce imaginative and slightly unconventional lessons for the children, who need a lot of stimulus. I think if I hadn't been crystal clear in my mind about the essence of history, then I might have been led to all sorts of vague and diffuse experiments − imaginative lessons which weren't really history; and I think I wouldn't have been able to do that sort of lesson with as much confidence and certainty if I had left W... at 21 and taken a certificate of education at 22.

A contrary view reflects the problem of the research student in a small department; she was in a separate department that covered a branch of history in a university that also had a main-line history department, and so she was working virtually on her own, cut off from other students with whom she had interests in common. Moreover, for only one student it is not worth providing a course of induction into the craft of historian.

ER. What do you think you got out of this period?
Not as much as I could have done. I now see that. I undoubtedly enjoyed myself. I did a lot of interesting work. But in terms of the academic skills that I acquired, there's a gap there. I think, with a different type of course, I could have become, at an earlier stage, a better type of historian. The teaching there boiled down to these occasional meetings with great minds; and also we had the ritual of the staff seminar, to which people came along, and one was supposed to sit and listen to someone talk about 16th century sheep-shearing or whatever. This was all part again of the way in which one learnt to be a historian I suppose.

PERSONAL DEVELOPMENT

The kind of gain that was most commonly mentioned was a general development of the mind and of personality. The general intellectual gains that were claimed, in contrast with the wide range of aspects of research from which people gained enjoyment were far more uniform. This comment came from a mature student still continuing his studies full-time:

It's very hard to say, because I'm still in the process of development but undoubtedly there has been a great deal of intellectual development. It's friends and outsiders who have said that. I can feel it myself. I have coped with things that I could not possibly have coped with before intellectually. I suppose I've got out of it what I wanted to get out of it. I'm also a happier man.

The next comment came from a student whose PhD thesis was with the examiners.

Oh what a question! The privilege to think, the time to think — that's something one didn't have as an undergraduate so much. I do feel I developed tremendously over the years. I think it's very good to give people a chance to test themselves intellectually to the extent they're testing themselves against their own standards, which I think is very valuable. And that's one of the reasons why I think tightening up in the way I would like to see would have to be done very carefully in terms of structuring a graduate school; because I don't think one should interfere with that. I think you should have to set your own standards, and you should have to see whether you can measure up to them and whether anyone else thinks your standards are any good.

It hasn't been a particularly pleasant process, but I think I gained a lot. I certainly gained, I think, my chief objective, which, as I said, was to find out what my limitations were; and I think in academic terms, and also because of the things that happened as far as my marriage was concerned, in more personal terms, I found out a lot about my limitations; and I think I've come out of the whole process a better human being that I was when I went in. Certainly people who knew me before and after the break-down of my marriage and giving up the thesis have said I'm much more human − that's the word they've used − since the process. People, especially local people, who are not particularly academically oriented, apparently regarded me as a kind of thinking machine.

Having completed that aesthetics course, I was perhaps a little less self-centred and selfish − perhaps less adolescent.

I think I became a less impetuous person during those three years than I had been as an undergraduate.

(The cynical might add that being over-impetuous is hardly the fault that first springs to mind in relation to these long-term students.)

It taught me quite a bit about myself, I suppose. It taught me that I'm reasonably self-motivating, but I'm not bursting with self-motivation − something I suppose I've always vaguely known because I tend to leave things to the last minute.

You have a problem at school or university, no one's really too bothered with you, it was an academic exercise in that everybody knew what the answer was already. It was a matter of whether you could get it out or not, and whether you were willing to put the time in to get the answer out; whereas for the PhD now, someone does mind whether you get the answer out because nobody does know what the answer to that particular problem is going to be. Now I think I tend to keep on until I get an answer. The piece of work I'm doing now, the answers won't just come out straight away. I think I've got the answers out now but it's taken a lot longer than I anticipated.

I got a tremendous amount out of the year that I did the MA thesis, because I worked away and I learnt how to work under my own direction, which I'd never done before, and I found I was capable of obsessive concentration on something, which was very new to me because I had been a very idle undergraduate; and I found I could work fast and work well and I lost a lot of my feelings of inferiority as a student. I realized I was quite good.

I learnt during two years as a research student, and carrying on from what I'd been learning as an undergraduate, the art of intellectual discourse and the art of critique. I think the way the Economics Department ran was very open, very conducive to taking questions, examining them from all points of view, criticizing established positions, formulating alternative positions. I think I learnt a great deal from that and from being able to exercise that not only with other research students but with very senior members of the department. I think the second thing I learnt was all kinds of personal skills, both as a research student and as a research officer at N..., which I find very useful now, skills like, for example, politics with a small 'p'.

These gains are very similar to those which university teachers I interviewed in an earlier study (Rudd 1975) claimed were produced by postgraduate research — indeed some would claim that such changes of character and personality are the main purpose of the research. Some students, however, differed from this view.

> To be frank with you, I started getting a bit bored with it as well, so I can't say I felt that I was really pursuing an academic scholarly topic which genuinely fascinated me and which I felt I gained an awful lot from intellectually, because I don't think I did.

> I'm not sure if I did get anything else out of it, and this is one of the regrets about the way in which I tackled research. I think I was expecting changes in me or in my outlook, and in fact the fairly isolated life that I led as a research student — I developed all kinds of social activities as well — but as a research student I have a suspicion that I stopped in the state I was in as an undergraduate at the end of my first degree.

A number of the students claimed that they had gained enhanced skills at writing.

> The ability to write at length — I was fairly well practised in that as an undergraduate, but obviously got more practice as a graduate.

> I did get more practice in writing. My English style isn't all it might be. I don't know if I'll ever end up writing anything much, apart from articles for parish magazines, which I've done.

Perhaps if more of them had gained this skill to a greater extent, more of them might have completed successfully.
   One kind of self-knowledge that some students had gained was, in my view, especially valuable.

> Perhaps I did get out of it too, the knowledge that, ultimately, this might not be what I was meant to be doing.

There were frequent references to the sense of achievement from completing an important stage of the work though, at times, it sounded a little like the sort of pleasure said to come from hitting one's head against a brick wall.

> When I finished going through all the correspondence — there were hundred and hundreds of letters — there was an enormous sense of satisfaction, saying 'Well, that's done'. But the other thing, I think, is just being immersed in it — understanding it, wallowing in it, enjoying it.

> I think I did a worth-while job for the Nature Conservancy. I'm pleased that I've been able to alter the course of events in one area for the better. I'm happy that I've been able to do that, and that would give me more satisfaction than anything else — to think that there was some area that I had turned my attention on to that was actually benefiting for more than a year or two. I think that's a marvellous thing to have achieved. I

obviously haven't got as far as I would like to have done, but the fact that I had even had a crack at it and had done some of the groundwork for somebody else to keep going is very satisfying.

ER. Do you feel you've got anything out of it?

I do now it's just nearing completion − I have been working on it all summer. I think I have a fairly large piece of work I put together entirely myself. The decision is largely my own about what's included and what's not included and I think I have developed a degree of independence.

The next comment came from a student who had recently submitted an MEd thesis:

I found a great deal of personal satisfaction when I saw this complete, submitted with the quality of a Readers' Digest publication.

Some of the satisfaction reported was beyond the reach of most of the people I interviewed − the satisfaction that somes from completing the work entirely.

Finally, a comment from someone who had recently gained a PhD, having been much delayed by a series of circumstances that had started with a serious injury.

Having finally got the piece of paper saying I've received the qualification, rather than just the esteem of colleagues who treated me as though I'd got it all along, having finally got the piece of paper, I recognize it did wonders for one's self-confidence − having people come up and say 'That's good; that's interesting stuff; where's it published?' And when the papers came out I received good comments about them. That's not just ego; it's self-confidence. You think, 'Yes, I've done something competent that's worth doing.'

Such a comment adds point to this whole study. Successful completion, by giving the student a new stature, encourages him to grow intellectually to fit that stature.

10

Fairness in the Examination of the Thesis

How fair is the examination procedure for a higher degree? I am sure that university examiners try hard to be both just and detached — when they disagree with the student on some controversial issue, they generally lean over backwards to be objective, and will sometimes carry this to the point of passing work which, but for this disagreement, would fail. But I find it hard to believe that everyone always succeeds in being so fair. Furthermore, given the very subjective nature of the decision on whether a thesis passes and the impossibility of specifying any absolute standard for a degree, there must be many marginal theses on which a different group of examiners would reach a different decision.

I have received a substantial body of letters and documentation from students who considered themselves aggrieved by the decisions on their theses, and some of these have managed to have their cases taken up by the national press. *The Times Higher Education Supplement* has had a series of letters from similar students. This is not surprising. What is more surprising is that there are so few such cases in relation to the numbers failing.

Perhaps some keep their feelings of injustice to themselves, knowing how hard it would be to convince other people, while, no doubt, other marginal students reluctantly accept the examiners' judgement. Those complaints that have surfaced have made some or all of the following points:

- The student had had no supervision, or bad supervision, and therefore had no knowledge of what level would be expected from a PhD thesis. If he had been better informed he would have spent longer on the thesis and covered enough ground to pass.
- The candidate had some evidence, generally a comment by a supervisor, that some other academics regarded the thesis as having reached an adequate level.
- There is no provision for an appeal to other judges (as distinct from re-submission to the same examiners).

One letter printed in the *THES* (from Liz Wells: 26.8.83) was allowed 30 column inches, a mark of editorial concern. Its typically tangled account of events was:

1 She held a research council award in the sociology department of the University of Bristol for two years.
2 During that time she took maternity leave.
3 She was not permitted to transfer her registration from a masters degree to a PhD.
4 She had good relations with her two supervisors.
5 When her grant ended, as her husband was a student, she had to find work.
6 Her husband then left her to live with a member of the Department's staff, which affected her own relationship with the staff.
7 She submitted her thesis, with the approval of her supervisors, some five years after she started work on it.
8 The external examiner referred her thesis for rewriting and resubmission.
9 In one case the rewriting would bring her thesis into line with her original intentions; she had modified this section on the advice of her supervisors.
10 She continued rewriting until told by the university that she would have to pay a fee of £116 to resubmit — she did not believe she could afford this sum.

Her comments covered a number of topics relating to the relationship between a student and a department. The points relevant to the fairness of the process of examination were:

− That no account was taken of personal factors, such as the strains caused by the way her marriage broke up.
− That there was no clear definition of the level of a masters.
− That one of her supervisors had expressed regret at not having recommended her for upgrading to a PhD registration, as she would then have failed her PhD but been awarded a masters; passing or failing should not depend upon the supervisors' tactics.
− That the process of learning is bound to produce a lack of harmony in a thesis as the student comes to realize the imperfections of the original research design and so the weakness of the work done in the early stages.

Regrettably, there is no way in which the staff concerned in a case of this kind can give their side of the story without a breach of confidence. However, the very moderate tone in which she told her story carries a measure of conviction, and the issues she and other correspondents raised, are undoubtedly relevant to the extent of the elements of chance and subjectivity in the whole process of examining candidates for higher degrees.

Seven of my sample had failed their examinations in that they had written examination papers for a masters degree and failed it, or had written a dissertation for a higher degree which had been failed, or, after submitting a thesis for a doctorate, had been awarded a masters degree. Of these, two had a strong sense of grievance. I have already referred, in various places, to one who, as a mature student, had been studying for a masters degree in literature. He attributed his failure to mainly ideological differences in attitudes to modern literature between himself and the staff, whom he regarded as very immature. Be this as it may, I am sure there were other causes, too, for his failure.

The other case was far more disturbing. An engineer, after a period in a large industrial firm, had worked for a PhD in a large engineering department, with money from both his employers and a research council. He took a little over three years to complete his thesis, submitting it, he said, with the approval of his supervisor. The department itself, following some changes in its leading staff, had started laying greater emphasis on theory than on the practical − other informants confirmed this. This meant that his supervisor's interests were out of fashion.

At an early stage in his research, the student applied for transfer from a masters degree to a PhD and his topic and detailed plans for the research were passed by the appropriate committee. When he submitted his thesis, he had, with one exception, done all the work specified in his plans. The exception was a relatively small part of his work, left aside, with his supervisor's agreement, to be completed later if there were time.

It is not the practice of his university to include the supervisor amongst the PhD examiners, but another member of the staff of the department, more junior than his supervisor, was the internal examiner, and the external examiner was a senior member of his employer's staff.

The internal examiner had had a student of his own working on a similar problem, but adopting a different approach to it, and had said that the approach being adopted by my informant and his supervisor would not work, whereas my informant said that it did in fact work. Also my informant said that his own relations with the internal examiner had not been good, especially as another student who was his closest friend used to have public rows with this member of staff.

Just before the oral examination, the external examiner asked him when he would be returning to their firm, and was told he would not be returning.

In the oral examination, the examiners concentrated especially on the part of the work that had not been completed. Also they seemed to imply that the project itself, however well done, could never be of PhD standard.

He was told to rewrite part of his thesis, and was then awarded an MPhil, which amounts to having failed. Word reached him in various ways that senior members of the staff of the department were disturbed at this decision.

I should add that, from various indications, I formed the impression that the student was of high ability.

Of course, there is no way in which I can check that the student's account is either complete or accurate. Nevertheless there is a *prima facie* case for inquiry into such a case, and that no such inquiry is possible must be a cause for concern. There are three especially worrying issues here.

The first is that a student may fail to gain a PhD not only through his own mistakes but also through those of his supervisor. My proposal for greater collective responsibility for the supervision of the student ought to reduce the risk of this; but the student's account of his examiners regarding as unsatisfactory a topic accepted by a committee on the basis of a carefully prepared and detailed research proposal is a reminder that no system can be perfect.

The second issue is one to which I have already referred. I have a suspicion that if the level of the PhD had remained at what a promising student could achieve in three years, he would have passed.

The third, and perhaps most serious, issue is that, although the student believed his examiners were influenced by personal hostility towards him, there was no satisfactory procedure by which he could appeal against their verdict. There is a need not only for justice to be done, which may or may not have happened in this case, but also for it to be seen to be done, for which the present procedures for the examination of PhD candidates make no provision. The only kinds of appeal open to a PhD candidate are those that are generally open to any student with a grievance; he can take a legal action against the university, or he can appeal to the University Visitor. Both are of little use to the aggrieved PhD student, as he would find it almost impossible to prove that he had been unfairly treated. Also a legal action is apt to be expensive.

A procedure for appealing against a degree result is far more necessary at higher degree that at first degree level. The decision on a first degree is usually an amalgam of a series of individual decisions by a number of markers, whereas that on a higher degree may rest almost entirely in the hands of the external examiners, of whom there may be only one. An essential feature of the appeals procedure should be a total re-marking by a completely fresh panel of examiners, who should not, if this can be avoided, know that they are reading a thesis that has already been failed by other markers.

11

What should be done?

WHAT ARE THE PROBLEMS?

The issues and problems which emerged in the course of the study and are illustrated in the foregoing extracts from interviews fall into eleven groups.

At the stage at which most students are deciding whether to enter postgraduate study, they know too little, for rational choice, about the options open to them. In particular, they rarely know enough about the difficulties of research, whether they will enjoy it and have an aptitude for it, what career they may realistically expect to follow from it, how much they will enjoy that career, what other options are available, and how much they would enjoy these.

Most of those who fail to complete a degree lack any very strong wish to do so − in the current jargon, they lack motivation. The only evidence for the stronger motivation of those who gain a degree is tautologous; they have surmounted the various hurdles so they must have wanted to surmount them. I do not think it should be discarded on that score; there is a great deal of common-sense in it.

The beginning of the road that leads to failure for many others is their choice of a research topic − either they choose a topic that is unsuitable for a postgraduate student, or they take too long over their choice, leaving themselves too little time for research.

Although the provision of courses introducing postgraduate students to the techniques of research has increased in recent years, especially in the natural sciences, many, especially in the arts and social sciences, still feel the lack of such instruction and either waste time, painfully discovering for themselves the techniques they need, or fail to master them.

Some students believe they have received incompetent or neglectful supervision, and in many cases I would judge that their claims are justified. Those minded to retort that I have heard only the students' side of the story should ask themselves whether they would claim that in university teaching there is an absence of the occasional incompetence and neglect of duties to be found in all other activities.

Some supervisors, not through incompetence or neglect, but through genuine conviction, are adopting procedures for supervision with which most of their colleagues would disagree and which decrease the likelihood of the student completing.

Those students who believe they are receiving incompetent or neglectful supervision can find no remedy for this.

Some students, though not lacking in other abilities, lack a flair for research. Others regard registration for a higher degree as an opportunity for dilettante reading and a fair measure of enjoyment of extended leisure — they do not lack motivation, only the motivation to do the disciplined work needed for a higher degree. They are able to enjoy themselves unchecked at public expense, taking up resources that others might have put to a better use.

Expectations of what students need to achieve to gain a PhD seem to have been rising, making it more difficult for a student to complete a successful thesis in the three years for which postgraduate studentships normally run.

If a student has not completed a PhD within three years, he will have increasing difficulty completing it at all. Also the stretching out of the time over which the results of the research are written up can, in some fields, mean that any published results would be of far less value.

There is no effective way in which a candidate for a research degree can appeal against the examiners' rejection of a thesis.

It is not my aim, in seeking solutions to these problems, to make the students happier. Indeed some of them, if more effectively supervised, so that sloppy work and laziness were not tolerated, would be far less happy.

SHOULD WE TRY TO FIND SOLUTIONS?

It could be argued that the problems, or difficulties, or even the trauma of graduate students reported in this book are on balance beneficial to them. New graduates still have much to learn and there are some things they can learn only from experience — for example what they enjoy doing, how they would prefer to spend the rest of their lives. Graduate study, whether successful or not, can give them that experience. It can also endow them with various skills, equipping them to make a greater contribution to society in whatever career or activity they follow. It could be argued that students would have learnt less, gained less from the experience, if their postgraduate studies had been easier and less traumatic. Linked to this is the point I make at the beginning of this chapter that some supervisors believe that leaving students to their own devices is the best way of ensuring that they learn to do research.

There certainly are many things that students cannot be taught or told. Few, for example, are prepared to listen to the advice that research is not for them, or that, though they might be successful in research, they would, eventually, regret that they had circumscribed their careers by taking it up. Although these are things they must learn for themselves, the way in which they do so could be improved. There is in particular a need to speed up the process, so that they go through this part of their exploration in the search for a career with less waste of their own time, of other people's time, and of public funds. The need for students to explore more quickly the choices before them is an argument against solutions to other research problems which, by making the PhD easier, enable the marginal student to hang on longer.

The arguments of those who say that students should be left to their own devices by their supervisors are somewhat different, and should not be treated with any the less respect or considered any the less carefully because they are sometimes a cloak for incompetence and neglect. Students can be over-supervised as well as under-supervised. If the supervisor does too much, it becomes his resarch rather than the students'. It is never difficult to find scientists who will tell you of the departments and fields where the research students are little more than pairs of hands.

That does not mean that students should be left almost entirely to their own devices – told that they can come to see their supervisors if they want help, but discouraged from doing so. If they are taught the more elementary aspects of research – the things that have already been learnt by others – they can make their own mistakes at a more advanced level, and so learn at a more advanced level. Descriptions of the Cavendish Laboratory in the days of J.J. Thompson and Rutherford stress how much they taught their research students; and there can have been few other laboratories at any time anywhere that produced so many world-class scientists. The description of his training given by Sir Hans Krebs – a Nobel laureate trained by a Nobel laureate who had himself been trained by yet a third – is another very different picture from that of a student left to discover most things for himself (Krebs 1967).

ENTRY TO POSTGRADUATE STUDY
Delayed Entry
Let us begin the search for solutions with three problems – that of most students' inability to make an informed choice from the options open to them before entering postgraduate study, that of sifting out those with insufficiently strong motivation for research, and that of a research student choosing a topic quickly with the risk of choosing the wrong one, or spending long on the choice and having too little time to.complete.

The first of these problems is especially intractable. An undergraduate research-project, which in a variety of shapes these days forms part of many, probably most, undergraduate schemes of study, may give the student some idea whether research is likely to be his métier. But I have known students whose undergraduate projects strongly indicated that research was not for them and who nevertheless were determined to enter research-oriented postgraduate study, which they did. Also, the PhD calls for qualities which cannot be adequately tested in the undergraduate research project; and the difference of scale alone is very substantial.

Although the academic staff ought to warn potential postgraduate students of the disadvantages of entering non-vocational postgraduate study, it is no use relying on this; not only are the students often unwilling to listen but many staff are unwilling to give the advice. Most of them believe strongly in the importance of research, and enjoy it, or, if they don't enjoy it, they probably won't admit it, even to themselves. So not only does the giving of advice of that kind go against the grain with them, but they do not accept that it is needed. And, as I said above, the discovery of what the student is good at comes only by trial and error.

The second problem, of sifting out the students with low motivation, is tied to the first, in that gaining the experience of doing research and discovering the enjoyment of it, together with the knowledge that it leads to an accessible and enjoyable career, are all things that will strengthen motivation, or whose absence will weaken it.

It might be argued that the solution of the third problem — providing the student with enough time for the choice of a topic without the risk of the research over-running the time available — is to extend studentships for a fourth year. Choosing a topic ought to include finding and reading a substantial amount of the relevant literature, and it can be argued that, as the literature has grown, the time needed for the literature search ought to be allowed to grow too. The Swinnerton-Dyer Working Party did recommend, albeit somewhat cautiously, a greater flexibility in allowing fourth years.

I do not believe the answer lies in that direction. Parkinson's law can be adapted to research — and not only to that done by research students — so that it reads 'Research expands to fill rather more time than is available for its completion'. P.M.S. Blackett's much quoted observation that, after the time to be taken by a piece of research has been estimated, it should be multiplied by the factor π, makes the same point.

The whole history of public support for research students in Britain shows that allowing them a longer period in which to complete their research is to give Danegeld — in another decade or so they will be back for more. It is in the students' interests to teach them to do research expeditiously for, at least in the social sciences, natural sciences and technology, that is how they will have to do it if they are to make a career in it. Therefore a solution to the problem must be found elsewhere. For the social sciences, the Swinnerton-Dyer Working Party recommended some reassessment of the nature of the PhD, or perhaps a new degree. This is an issue to which I return below. However, I think another change is needed — one that I believe would make a substantial contribution, not only in speeding research without making it merely second-rate and pedestrian, but also in eliminating those students who should not enter in the first place.

Because of the greater diversity of taught courses, the problem of students on these is in some ways more complicated, and so I look at that separately below.

My suggestion is that UK students (other than those employed as research assistants on group research) should not be admitted to full-time study for a research degree until they have completed their initial search of the literature and written a carefully thought-out and detailed research proposal. They would do this initial work in their spare time, registered as part-time students. While doing it, they would be under the supervision of members of the university's staff, who would have to be prepared to see them in the evenings and at week-ends. Preliminary courses of instruction relevant to the planning of research would be so phased that they could be attended by part-time students. Other preliminary courses, especially those relating to highly specialized techniques needed in specific areas of research, would come better at the beginning of the full-time research.

Some way would have to be found either of registering these students without fees, or paying their fees from public funds, and they might need small grants for fares and other minor expenses.

In effect, this is a requirement that people should provide clear evidence of aptitude and suitability for research before they become full-time research students supported by public funds. A publisher who handed out advance royalties for novels on the strength of performance in a degree exam and a brief interview would soon go bankrupt — but that is very similar to what we do when giving away money for research degrees.

It also requires students to make a conscious decision that they wish to enter postgraduate education either because it is relevant to the career they have started or because trying other careers has reinforced a determination to do research. Making them start as part-time students when in employment will test their determination and will eliminate those who would not be prepared, at the end of the full-time study, to complete the degree in their spare time.

It is an essential part of this scheme that the preparation of the research proposal, and the student's examination on it, should be treated as seriously as a PhD examination. Its purpose would be to determine whether the student showed sufficient promise — a sufficient likelihood of success — to be admitted to full-time study for a research degree. The student would be orally examined on his proposal to make sure that he really understood what he was trying to do and was not just putting forward plans drawn up by the supervisor. For this reason, and others too, the supervisor should not be a member of the interviewing panel, though he should have a veto over a decision to admit. It might be useful to appoint an external examiner to the panel.

Many students at present studying for research degrees would not go far under such a system. Some would find the prospect of two or even three years of part-time study before beginning research too daunting and so would not even start, while others would give up during this period, through discovering that they value their leisure too much to want to continue, or that they can find a satisfying career to which a research degree is irrelevant, or both.

At the same time, the scheme would enable students who do not have first class or upper second class Honours degrees to become research students — the rigorous procedure I am suggesting for admission to full-time study ought to satisfy the research councils, the DES and the SED, and so replace the present requirements for eligibility for a studentship. This would open access to a doctorate to some potentially good but hitherto ineligible students. The class of first degree is a poor predictor not merely of whom to accept for a research degree, but also of whom to reject.

Amongst those who successfully completed this preliminary stage, some would stay in employment, either continuing their research as part-time students or using work done for their employers for a research degree; this would give more of an applied slant to the research entered for higher degrees.

Choice of Topic

My suggestion for revised entry qualifications implies that the student would take a rather more active role in the selection of his research topic, whereas the Swinnerton-Dyer Working Party seem to have wanted to swing the balance a little the other way; though it is difficult to be sure of this as their perception of the present position was clouded by their use of the PSI survey (Whalley 1982). In some cases at present, both the student and the supervisor will agree that the topic is the student's idea, and in some they will both agree that the topic came from the supervisor, but in many cases, if the supervisor and the student are asked separately, each will say he thought of the topic. This third case seems to me the ideal, as it implies that both the student and supervisor took an active part in the choice of the topic, and both feel a sense of commitment to it.

The balance between the parts played by the supervisor and by the student varies from field to field, with the supervisor having more influence in science and technology, and less in the humanities and social sciences. Also older students are likely to contribute more to the search for their topic than those who come straight from a first degree.

In principle no one could dissent from what the Swinnerton-Dyer Working Party said here, which they summarize as:

> ... the choice of research topic should be heavily influenced by the staff and, where appropriate, also from outside the academic institution; this is to ensure that the topic is a suitable subject for research training, that it is likely to prove rewarding in investigation, that it is of practical benefit where this is possible, that competent supervision is available and that the work can be completed within the time available.

One can, however, object to three omissions; first, that learning to choose a topic for research, and to distinguish those on which useful and significant results are likely to be achieved within the time available, is part of a training in research, secondly, that if the student has not actively taken part in the choice of his research topic, he may not have an adequate sense of commitment to it; and thirdly, that if a student wants to do research that cannot be satisfactorily done or supervised where he is, but can be elsewhere, he should have the choice either of moving or of changing his topic.

Under the present arrangements, it is, in theory, possible for a student to move at an early stage of his research; but in practice moves hardly ever occur except between graduation and taking up a postgraduate studentship. Under my scheme it would be far easier for the student to move. If, during the working-out of his proposal, it became clear that someone else in the department would be better able to supervise him, he would be passed on within the department; but if his interests shifted outside the areas the department could satisfactorily supervise, he could be transferred elsewhere quite easily. His studentship would not yet have begun, so the many obstacles and difficulties in the way of moving during a studentship, and especially the feeling that the department would lose a quota award, would not arise.

Indeed, the adoption of this scheme, together with others that I outline below, ought to reduce the number of cases where a member of staff persuades himself that he is capable of supervising a research topic that he really ought to pass on elsewhere. It also ought to reduce the number of cases where a scientist or technologist sets out to do research in a department that lacks the necessary equipment; though, in this case, in addition to the possibility of going to a different department, if a suitable one can be found, there is also the possibility of postponing the beginning of the research until the equipment has been bought – at present many science and technology students waste time waiting for equipment.

However, a more important consideration is that the student who manages to produce a research proposal that is viable and of high quality before he begins his research should, after that, be able to finish the research, the writing-up and the revision well within three years of full-time study.

Entry to Group Research

I said above that I did not intend my scheme for the selection of students and their topics to apply to research assistants attempting to gain a higher degree through contribution to the group research on which they were employed. For them, the need to find their own research problem clearly does not arise. The form the research will take will have been worked out before they arrive, and it will have been submitted to the normal process of peer-review before funds were provided for it.

There is still, of course, the problem of selecting for the assistantship someone who is likely to be successful at research. Here, again, it is different from choosing a research student. For the senior members of the research team, more is at stake when they are selecting an assistant than when they are admitting a student, and they can be expected to consider the candidate's suitability more carefully, perhaps preferring a candidate with some research experience and of proven ability to one of their own newly graduated students.

Other problems that arise in group research will be discussed below.

Entry to Taught Courses

Taught courses can be divided into four categories:

1 Courses that are a prerequisite for entry to a career, including conversion courses. These may turn a mathematician or economist into a statistician, a chemist or civil engineer into a chemical engineer, a psychologist into a clinical psychologist, or an arts graduate into a personnel manager.
2 Courses to permit a graduate who is already trained for a career to become more specialized within that career. Many courses in engineering are of this kind.
3 Up-dating courses, intended to inform people with special interests about the latest developments and advances of knowledge within their field.
4 Courses that are broadly educational rather than specifically vocational. Most courses in the arts, and many in the social sciences come into this group.

Of these, only the first category seems to need to come immediately after a first degree. However, even here some of the courses — for example in librarianship and clinical psychology — require students to gain some relevant experience before entry. The second category, which at present often admits new graduates, would seem, logically, to come far better after the graduate has gone sufficiently far into his career to know with fair certainty on what he intends to specialize; and he is unlikely to know that until he has actually worked for a while.

The third category is best taught by whatever choice from, or mixture of, very short full-time courses, longer part-time courses, or distance teaching suits the people at whom the course is aimed, who will usually be in employment.

The fourth category presents more difficulties. It is used, even more than research, as a refuge by graduates who know what they have to do – go out and find a job – but do not want to do it yet. I said above that failures on such courses generally occur at the stage at which a research project has to be carried out and written up, so that the reasons for failure are often similar to those of research students. As, however, the research is not the main part of the course but something which follows from the taught element, it would not be practical, and indeed would be wholly inappropriate, to base entry to such courses on the writing of a research proposal. Nevertheless, it would, in this case, as in research, eliminate some of the less strongly motivated from the entry if they had to interpose a couple of years or so between graduation and a course before they could join it.

Will these Changes ever come?

It would be completely unrealistic to expect any university to introduce these changes of its own accord. The major obstacle is that what I am suggesting would, intentionally, reduce the intake into postgraduate study. Indeed, unless the new system were introduced gradually over a period, there would be hardly any entry at all for two or three years, with unacceptable consequences for the staffing of universities. But even if that difficulty were solved, there would still be strong objections to the long-term reduction in numbers.

University staff may accept, intellectually, that though their scholarship and research are of importance to society others may see a whole host of things as at least equally important. But when their world is under attack they try hard to hang on to whatever they have got. And it is difficult for them to accept that their building up of postgraduate study has gone too far for the good of either the students or the country.

Therefore, if these changes are to come at all, the initiative must be taken by the bodies giving studentships – the research councils, the DES and the SED. It will be difficult for them, too, to accept that they have gone too far in the production of higher-degree graduates – the Swinnerton-Dyer Working Party clearly found it impossible to believe it. But eventually the clear message of the data about the demand for higher-degree graduates will have to be accepted – indeed the ending of the rise in numbers of awards some years ago (about 1972) and the slight falls of recent years suggest that the message has already begun to be received, at least at the Treasury. My fear is that, in the absence of a university initiative, the research councils may react to increasing pressure on their funds simply by cutting numbers and not by imposing the changes in structure that I have suggested.

Certainly the award-giving bodies, if they acted together, would have the power to impose this change for home students – if they made it a condition of support that the student should have been examined on a research proposal, the universities would have to introduce the necessary procedures.

The overseas students are a separate problem, if only because they could not be expected to study part-time while working out a research proposal. However, not only are the overseas students older than the home students, but in no way could most of them be described as having drifted into postgraduate study, and they are far more strongly motivated. Therefore most of my scheme would be irrelevant to their problems. They would still benefit, however, from working out a research proposal on which they would be examined before they were allowed to start research, even though they would do it as full-time students.

THE ORGANIZATION OF SUPERVISION
The Problems
I must make it clear at the outset that the problems in supervision I have been describing should not be regarded as the normal state. I have no doubt that most supervisors are reasonably conscientious and competent, and that most graduate students are hard-working, but it is precisely when one of the pair is not hard-working, conscientious and competent that the problems arise, or, sometimes, the student and the supervisor simply do not get on with one another, or there is a genuine difference of opinion, in which the supervisor may not always be right. An example of a wide range of other causes of uneasy relationships was the case I reported above, of a student who believed his results and findings were being used by the supervisor for his own research.

Where the student is dissatisfied with the supervisor, there is generally, as I said in Chapter 8, nothing he can do about it. Most students feel that a complaint carries slight chance of gain, and near certainty of substantial loss. Where the supervisor is dissatisfied with the student, more is likely to be done about it; but it is difficult for a member of staff enjoying friendly relations with a graduate student to be really horrid to him, however much it may be needed, and especially difficult to take the ultimate step of recommending that the student should be thrown out and his studentship terminated. Indeed this last grave sanction should not be in the sole power of any one person.

A student attending a taught course is generally in touch with a number of members of staff who have taught him, and is rarely in the state of dependence on one person that allows these problems to develop and fester. For the research student, however, an independent arbiter is called for, who will keep an eye on the way the student and the supervisor are progressing. To be effective the arbiter must be someone such as a chairman, head of department of dean who can be approached by either the student or the supervisor. But even though chairmen and deans are around at present, it is clear that many cases on which they ought to be taking action are not brought to them. What is needed is some person, body or organization that will, at regular intervals, take the initiative in looking searchingly at the progress of the student and his research.

Supervisory Committees
In a few departments within a few universities such a body exists in the shape of a supervisory committee appointed for each research student, or, sometimes, for all the research students in a department. At its best, the system provides for regular, once-a-term sessions at which student and supervisor appear, separately, and are questioned on reports they have submitted on the student's progress. If it does nothing else, such a system

ensures that the student sits down to think about his research and write something about it at regular and reasonably frequent intervals, and that the supervisor, at similar intervals, makes sure he knows how the student is progressing. But it can do a great deal more than this. The members of the supervisory committee can question the student sufficiently intensively to discover if he is making adequate progress, and, if not, to form an opinion why. They can look very intently to see if anything is going wrong and take corrective action if it is.

The committee should be entirely aware that it is not merely extending a helping hand to the student and supervisor, but is also, to a certain extent, sitting in judgement on both. It must be prepared to intervene in a thoroughly ungentlemanly manner, even if this means upsetting a colleague. And it must be composed, or at least include a substantial element, of more senior staff, both so that there can be no question of a senior supervisor being able to override the criticism of a committee of more junior staff and because it is essential that the members of the committee should themselves be experienced and competent supervisors.

An additional advantage of the supervisory committee system is that if the supervisor goes on study-leave, resigns, becomes seriously ill, or falls prey to the other chances of this mortal life there are a number of other members of staff with some knowledge of the student and his work who could replace him. Also there will be at all times a concerned body of people to whom the student can go for help and advice.

I made available to the Swinnterton-Dyer Working Party a note, written for my own university, recommending the setting up of supervisory committees; and they came, perhaps independently, to the same conclusion about the need for them.

The system is not, however, the perfect panacea for all that can go wrong with a student's research. A chairman of a department that does have supervisory committees told an SRHE Leverhulme conference that a careful count had shown that its introduction had not improved his department's rate of completion. There are a number of possible explanations for this — that the kind of department that introduces such committees may be the kind that needs them least, that it is dangerous to draw conclusions from small numbers, or that, but for the committees, the completion rate might have fallen, as it may well have done in other departments. But the most simple point is that, although supervisory committees may reduce the incidence of certain kinds of failure, and perhaps improve the quality of passes, they will not totally prevent such failures. Moreover, if their intervention causes a student who is not really working, or who is barely coping, to leave, the completion rate may actually decline. Also, part of the committees' importance lies in an ability to sort out the especially distressing and intractible problems.

Two women students told me that they had found it easy to pull the wool over the eyes of their committees, making it seem that their work was going much better than it really was. The fact of their being women is significant here. I suspect some all-male committees do not know how to deal with a woman who is putting on an act. They were probably not fooled at all, but did not quite know how to cope with the situation, and were in any case too gentlemanly to apply the harshness that was needed. Also, they only saw the student, I believe, once a year, which is not often enough. If they had seen her every few weeks they would not have been able so easily to ignore the problem, or to forget about it.

The committees, as gatherings of ordinary humans, will have their failures too. There is no perfect system, and it is useless to imagine one can be found. That such committees should always be appointed everywhere seems to me, however, to be one way of improving a very imperfect system.

Introductory Courses

Important as they are, the appointment of supervisory committees should be seen as only one of several steps that many departments can take to improve their teaching of graduate students. For a start, departments should look at their provision of introductory instructional courses. I wonder how many departments have thought to ask their research students what courses they have found useful, or might have found useful if they had been provided?

Appointment of Supervisors

Another area needing attention is in the appointment of supervisors. It should not be assumed that any member of staff can supervise a research student. As the students I saw said, the supervisor should himself either have gained a PhD or written a major comparable work. I would go much further. In my view it is essential that the supervisor should have done first-rate research – not just the rather pedestrian work that often gets by for a PhD. Secondly, they should have had extensive research experience, going very substantially beyond the completion of the one good piece of research needed for the PhD – if they have not had this breadth of experience how can they possibly guide anyone whom they cannot clamp into their own narrow area of expertise (as the supervisors of some of my informants had tried to do)? In addition, they need an adequate knowledge of the literature, both in and around the student's field, a wide and deep grasp of the subject, and flexibility of mind. After this come those personal qualities sought by the student. No amount of compatibility can compensate for the failure to supervise the student's research properly, giving sound advice as and when it is needed.

Here there is a conflict between what the student initially wants when seeking a supervisor and what is good for him. The extensive experience of research which I regard as essential cannot possibly be found in the younger members of a department's staff (that is, of course, when departments have younger members, for, although these are rare today, I regard this as a temporary phenomenon). However, Welsh (1979) has found that at the outset of their research students prefer to be supervised by the younger members of staff, with whom they find it easier to establish a comfortable and friendly relationship.

Of course, everyone wants the student to be happy. But it is far less comfortable to have one's ideas searchingly questioned than to have them let alone. Students are unlikely to feel that they can relate easily to a supervisor who is intolerant of sloppy thought. Therefore there is a conflict between the student's short-term satisfaction with a supervisor who is closer to him in age and his longer-term satisfaction with a supervisor who can give him adequate supervision.

The choice, however, is not merely between inadequate supervision in a friendly atmosphere or more exacting supervision in one that is less comfortable. Some departments seem to find an even worse alternative – the handing out of students, or at least of the studentships that will bring a student, on the basis of fair shares for everyone. Regardless of competence to supervise the particular research student, or even research students in general, everyone must have a student. This represents a total subjection of the interests of the students to those of the staff.

I do not know how often departments give to the choice of a supervisor the kind of careful consideration it should have, with the student's interests, as distinct from what he requests, made paramount. I do not know how often departments' recommendations of supervisors are given a thorough and critical scrutiny by deans, or whoever is required to approve such appointments. Frequently, I hope. All I am sure of is that there are numerous cases where this does not happen.

Group Research

It is tempting to see in group research a solution to the problem of inadequate supervision. In theory, and sometimes in practice, the student who is part of a group consisting of teaching staff, research staff and students is in contact so continuously with a range of other people that the kinds of problems that lead to many other students giving up are solved as they arise. However, as I have pointed out above, though group research can prevent the onset of some of the problems that arise in solo research, it does not always do so. Some research groups have a rigid and hierarchical structure which may cut the student off from being able easily to seek advice from the staff in other sections. And there are likely to be cliques, factions and jealousies, unless the head of the group has good powers of leadership, and sensitivity, and is able to inspire the group with a unifying sense of common purpose.

In addition, group research brings certain difficulties which are absent from solo research. The student may find himself diverted from work which will give him usable research results and onto trouble-shooting or the production of minor items of hardware or software to produce results for others. Here there is a conflict between the group's need for results and the student's progress towards a degree, as well as perhaps his training. There can also be conflict with his ability to produce the kind of research results that are sufficiently his own, and sufficiently connected, to form a PhD thesis, which problem I will turn to below, when I discuss the structure of the PhD.

The problems of group research seem to me to suggest that, here too, there is a need for some body of people regularly and frequently to look at the student's progress, questioning him on it, and trying to eliminate obstacles to his completing the degree. The difficulty could well lie in finding people who are sufficiently independent of whatever pressures within the group are impeding the student's progress, and sufficiently influential to see that these are removed.

Though, as I have pointed out, group research has some weaknesses as a road to a research degree, and is certainly not the panaca for all the ills of research training, I do not want to minimize its very substantial strengths. It is the form of research in which many graduates will be employed, so it is a form of research in which they need to be trained. It provides the researcher's equivalent of the form of industrial training sometimes called 'sitting next to Nelly' — learning to do the job by doing it alongside someone with long experience and considerable skill in it. It gives the student the opportunity to engage in a wider range of tasks than he is likely to meet in solo research. Problems of supervision are less likely to occur in group than in solo research. And, perhaps most important of all, in many fields it is only the substantial groups that can made significant contributions to knowledge, and it is only membership of such a group that offers the student the experience of joining in such advances. A student who has had this experience ought not to be content with the trivial, pedestrian work that so often passes for research.

However, it is easier to say that students ought to engage in group research than to ensure that they actually do it. As I pointed out to the Swinnerton-Dyer Working Party, an increase in the pressure towards group research is more likely to result in changes of nomenclature than in real changes in the way in which research students are trained. I will give two illustrations. The first is a department, to which I have referred above, from which I interviewed several students. Part of the department had named itself a research group, which had probably helped it gain grants on a generous scale from the SERC. The students' descriptions of their research made it clear that it was not what would normally be regarded as group research. Contacts between the students, and between students and staff, seemed no closer than they would be in any large department with a substantial number of students.

The second illustration comes from one of the surveys commissioned by the Swinnerton-Dyer Working Party (Whalley 1982). This included a question in more than usually loose wording in which departments were asked:

> In general, do PhD students tend to work on their individual topics within a framework of closely integrated research groups, or within looser groupings having some common research interests, or do they on the whole tend to work as separate, unrelated units?

Given that it was well known that the research councils favoured group research, it was not surprising that departments stretched the rather elastic phrase 'loose groupings having some common research interests' as far as it would go, and returned an unbelievable 87 per cent of departments in the social sciences, physical and biological sciences and engineering whose students were engaged in group research.

If the research councils want to increase the percentage of students taking part in group research they will need to do more than announce this policy and give favour to departments claiming to be implementing it. After all, all the research students in a department of electronics are doing research on electronics; so any department with more than one student could claim its students are working on related topics and thus forming a research group. The research councils will need to look extremely searchingly at the research actually done by students within 'groups', and even take the unethical step of asking students about the extent and nature of their collaboration with staff and fellow students.

Perhaps the most effective way the research councils could stop departments from dressing up all their research as group research would be to stop awarding studentships for students taking part in group research, and, instead, regard the provision of research assistantships for research supported by grants, where the grant was given to a substantial group, as a way of providing a training in research. It would be easier then to provide funds for whatever period of time was needed to complete the research; and the senior researchers would be more likely than the supervisor of a research student to make sure that work which they would regard as their own research really was completed.

THE SUPERVISOR'S TASK

I am sure many university staff will have read this far with a mounting sense of reassurance. On the one hand they have not recognized as theirs any of the major faults of supervisors mentioned by students. They are not, for example, involved in feuding within their departments, which could (if they were) harm their students. They have never failed to turn up for appointments with their students. ("'What *never*?" "Hardly ever!'" − Gilbert 1878). On the other hand, most of my suggestions cover wide areas of policy over which they may feel, somewhat thankfully, that they have no say.

Nevertheless, it seems worth noting what tasks my sample's supervisors seem most commonly to have neglected, even though supervisors have recently been offered plenty of sound advice, widely applicable across all fields, in booklets on supervision published by both the SERC (Christopherson 1982) and the ESRC (ESRC 1984b).

Leaving aside inexperience, the lack of some personal quality essential to a supervisor, and negligence, those major faults of supervision that seem to me to have emerged from my interviews are:

1 Over-zealous recruitment to postgraduate studies.
2 Failure to help the student find a topic that can be completed in the time available.
3 Lack of an overall plan, coupled with allowing the student to spend far too long on each stage of the research.
4 Failure to keep sufficiently closely in touch with the student and to ensure that he is working steadily.
5 Allowing the student to postpone writing up, and to flounder over it.

In bringing together the threads of earlier chapters to weave something of use to supervisors, it is easy to fall into two traps. The first is to offer advice that, though sound, is useless, such as 'Avoid allowing your marriage to break up. The strain would affect your work and so harm your students.' The second is to offer advice at so general a level that it tells the reader nothing.

Head-hunting or Motivation

My first advice is likely to be the most unpalatable; staff should stop head-hunting for postgraduate students from amongst their graduates.

Instead they should be giving their students advice that is realistic in the sense that it enables them to judge more accurately the likely effect of postgraduate study on their careers. What this should be must depend to a certain extent on the student's subject, but there are some points that should almost always be made.

If the student is thinking of taking up research, the first thing to do is to remove the aura of glamour and make sure the student realizes that research is difficult, lonely and generally frustrating, that much of it is dull routine, and that the moments of triumph come only rarely and to a few, completely eluding many. They should be disabused of the idea that the years of low income as students will bring them high income later. Instead it will only condemn them to a relatively low income later, as research, compared with other graduate occupations, is relatively low-paid.

They should also be made aware that the likelihood of a job in a university or polytechnic, even for a graduate with a first and a PhD, is now virtually nil, whereas there are many other openings for a graduate with a first only.

Students who are thinking of taking a taught course should be made aware that the regulations for grants limit the number of years' support for postgraduate study that can be given to any individual, and in some cases they should be urged to consider carefully whether it is better to take up further study immediately or to defer it until, having started a career, they know better what kind of further study will be of most benefit to them.

Most students will brush aside all such advice, saying that research is still what they want to do, and that they are prepared to accept the effect on their job prospects and careers. (This will not, of course, stop them moaning, three years later, about the lack of university jobs.) But advice of this kind might, by deterring a few of the less motivated students, go a little way towards eliminating potential drop-outs.

Choosing the Topic

I assume that the student already knows what kind of work he wants to do. Then there are three main parts to the supervisor's task here. First, he needs to be able to see areas not only where research can be done but where it needs to be done, where it offers some chance of making a significant contribution to knowledge. The student should not be trained to do trivial research.

Secondly, the supervisor needs to be able to stimulate the student into finding a subject from within such areas. It must be one that attracts the student, who must take an active part in hammering it out for himself. It is important the student should not be a passenger at this stage; otherwise he may be like the student who told me of listening to his supervisor outlining a topic without really understanding what was being said to him. If he cannot show some ability for independent thought at this stage, why expect him to achieve it later?

Thirdly, the supervisor needs to be able to judge how much can be done within the time available to the student, and to guide him into so shaping the project that it will be done. The basic problem is that to predict accurately the time the research will take it is necessary to foresee all the difficulties that will arise and how they can be overcome; and if it is possible to do that at the outset the research cannot be truly original. In the social sciences, at least, it is not only students' research that has been left uncompleted when the work took longer than was originally planned. Although, in time, the professional researcher becomes skilful at guessing how long a particular piece of research will take, success lies not merely in making a good guess but also in knowing how to adapt the plans when the guess proves to have been wrong.

This brings me to the third major problem.

The Need for an Overall Plan

Virtually all my informants told me they had never discussed with their supervisors the overall planning of their research and its timing. This is at first sight especially surprising, for anyone applying for a research grant is familiar with the need to work out carefully how long each stage of the research will take. Perhaps the supervisors had never applied for a research grant.

However, the drawing-up of an overall timetable for a student's research differs from that for any other type of research. When planning research for a grant application, one begins at the beginning, working out how long each successive stage will take. For a student's research, the planning should start at the other end, allowing for the time needed for writing-up — for a PhD in the sciences perhaps six to nine months; for a PhD in the arts and social sciences nine months to a year. Next the time needed for the research has to be estimated, and what is left is the time available for the literature survey and planning. If the time left for these is too short, the size of the research project has to be reviewed and adjusted.

Next each of the main stages has to be subdivided, and a time allotted for each, so that the student knows when he should be moving from one phase of the work to another. This timetable should be written down, so that both student and supervisor can check from time to time to see how closely they are keeping to it.

The first sketching out of a plan and a timetable should take place at the very outset of the research. This may make it clear that there are too many unknowns for the plan to be realistic. The most likely discovery is that the student needs to do a more substantial amount of reading and other exploratory work before he can formulate his research topic. In that case, the supervisor should encourage the student to go away and do something else for a year or two, putting his spare time into exploring around his proposed research, so that, when he comes back, he will be able to draw up firmer plans. (The supervisor will also, of course, need to negotiate the agreement to this of the research council or department supporting the student.)

Inevitably, the research will not keep entirely to the planned timetable, and it is in the way in which they react to this that the better supervisors differ from the others. The falling away from the timetable may be due to unexpected difficulties, and any supervisor will be trying to help his student find a way around these. It may also be simply that a particular kind of work, or stage of the work, takes longer than expected, in which case the supervisor needs to discover why it is taking longer, and guide the student into ways of working faster. However, it may also be that the student finds the way ahead blocked: the experiment simply cannot be made to work, someone else has done similar research already, permission for access to the data has been refused, there is too little material in the archives, etc.

All these problems exemplify the need for supervisor and student constantly to have in their heads a range of alternative plans and strategies, and constantly to consider ways of modifying the original plan so that the work will still be finished in time. This is one of the skills in which I believe supervisors differ most.

Keeping in Touch

It is very easy to keep at the back of one's mind for a long time the need to do a piece of work, while finding other things to do that seem more pressing. This amounts to culpable neglect when the work postponed is a supervisor's session with a research student. Few of the supervisors of my sample seem to have taken the simple way out by arranging a series of regular dates for supervisions from the start of the research. Where they had, it was sometimes the student who resented and resisted it because he found he had nothing to report to his supervisor. But the student having nothing to report is a significant fact needing the supervisor's attention.

That student and supervisor work in adjoining labs and are constantly meeting is no reason not to timetable regular meetings for a thorough review of progress. Apart from any other consideration, neither may be noticing how fast the pages of the calendar are turning.

Regular Writing

If the student is to be able to move smoothly into the phase of continuous writing, it is essential that he should start writing working papers and drafts as early as possible. It is not merely that he needs constant practice at writing, but also that the task of writing clears the mind, showing where there are gaps in one's thinking and problems that have just not been faced.

Moreover, seeing written work regularly and discussing it with the student provides a hinge for the supervision, giving the supervisor a clearer idea of progress and alerting him to points on which the student needs help and advice. It may, for example, show up muddled thinking and a lack of clarity about the objectives of the research; or it may show that the student has not mastered the problem of taking notes and keeping records in a form that lends itself to convenient use. It was clear to me that many of the students I saw were better at putting things into box files than at getting them out. Furthermore, seeing written work is the best way to judge progress, as there is less scope for fluffing in the written than in the spoken word.

Many students already have regular supervisions at which they discuss written work with their supervisors. It was clear from my interviews that some of the others would resent this — this is another example of the gap that can develop between what the student wants and what he needs. Where, as will often be the case, the student's resentment flows from having achieved too little, and so having too little to report, the supervisor should not let the situation drag on to the inevitable failure, but should recommend that the student's registration be terminated.

SANCTIONS AGAINST INSTITUTIONS

The Swinnerton-Dyer Working Party recommended that a graded series of sanctions should be taken against universities and polytechnics with low completion rates. The ultimate sanction would be to withhold quota awards.

I am far from opposed to sanctions. As Dr Johnson said of one ultimate sanction: it 'concentrates the mind wonderfully', and I doubt if universities will really tackle thoroughly the problem of low completion rates without some such sanctions being at least threatened. Indeed, I wish I were convinced that they will do this even with the sanctions.

However, I feel I should point out three pitfalls. The first is the risk that, as departments will know that every failure to complete will count against them, they will not throw out the idle or incompetent student who should not be allowed to continue, but will, instead, keep him on, hoping it will all turn out alright in the end, even if the supervisor has to write most of the thesis himself.

There are ways round this, such as excluding students thrown out during the currency of their awards from the calculation of completion rates, or even giving departments especially good marks for throwing out students with good reason − though this might be a little extreme; departments should be encouraged to solve their problems, where possible, by less drastic methods.

The second pitfall is that there are probably few institutions, as opposed to departments or subjects, with bad records. I calculated the rank order correlation for the institutions which appeared in the lists prepared (for the Swinnerton-Dyer Working Party) by both the SERC and the SSRC, setting out institutions in the order of their completion rates (or at least the lists as leaked to *The Times*). I found there was a small negative correlation between the two lists − in other words, universities that had a high completion rate on one list were slightly more likely to have a low than a high completion rate on the other list.

The third pitfall is that an excessive concentration on success rates could encourage departments to stick to those topics that are completely safe because it is entirely predictable that they can be solved. This could result in an intensification of the present tendency for pedestrian researchers to produce yet more pedestrian researchers. We have enough of these. It is the original and creative researchers we need, and I doubt if they can be trained on predictably soluble problems.

THE FORM AND NATURE OF THE PhD
The Problems
I have skated rapidly over two issues relevant to the form and nature of the PhD. The first is the apparent tendency for the level of work required for success to rise, and, correspondingly, for the time students take to complete to increase.

The second issue arises from the problem of finding, from within the work done by a research group, an adequate amount, attributable to the student's own efforts, which can be written up in a sufficiently coherent and consecutive manner to form his thesis.

Publications instead of a Thesis
I suggested to the Swinnerton-Dyer Working Party that a solution of the second problem would be to make more use of a procedure already available, to a limited extent, in some universities, by which a candidate for the PhD can submit his publications in lieu of a thesis. There is also a wider

case for extending such an arrangement. If universities are training researchers and the normal mode of communication of research results is an article, it makes sense to train students to produce articles and to measure their success by the extent to which they have carried out research that has been accepted for publication.

The Working Party made what seems, at first sight, to be a reasonable reply. They said, in effect, that in science and technology one necessary method of communicating research results is the research report, that most of the employers of graduates expect them to write these, and that, unlike graduates in the social sciences, science and technology graduates gain no practice in writing lengthy pieces of connected prose as undergraduates. Therefore they had to be trained to do this as research students, and it was reasonable to require them to do it in their submission for the PhD.

However, it seems to me likely that most science graduates, and not merely those destined for research, need, for their future work, to be able to write extended pieces of prose. Indeed, many of those who will not enter research but will go instead into management and administration will need this skill more than will the researchers. Therefore there is a case for fostering the skill in the undergraduate course. To use the PhD to provide this training is not merely inadequate, in that it leaves many graduates without it, but is also using a steam-hammer to crack a nut.

As undergraduate students normally produce more written work in the social sciences, the Working Party did not think there was the same argument there for the role of the thesis in the PhD, and in that context they added: 'we think the idea deserves serious consideration'.

The Working Party's comments on the remaining problems of group research are best taken in two parts. First they commented on the consequences of the end-product of the student's efforts sometimes being a piece of apparatus or a program. I would add, in passing, that, especially in science or technology, something of that kind can be the end-product of a student's research even when he is not taking part in anything that can, except by the loosest definition, be described as group research. I found a similar case in the humanities where the end-product would be an interpretation by performance of the intentions of a composer of early music. They said that, in such cases, the thesis could consist of a description of the problems that the student had to face, and how they were overcome, together with a description of the end-product. This is, I believe, what is already happening.

The more important and awkward problem is how students can write an account of their research when there is hardly anything of any substance in the work of the team that is the achievement of any one person alone. The extent of this problem varies from group to group. At the edge of group research, the student may work for his three years on a single problem that forms part of the group's programme; and all sorts of variations are to be found between that and fully integrated team-work where no one does by himself more than a little of this and a little of that. It is at this extreme that the larger problems arise.

The Working Party said that it might be difficult, when it came to writing PhD theses, 'to isolate each individual's contribution to the group and to pretend that it constitutes an identifiable piece of research.' This problem they virtually dismissed, assuming that there would be something in the joint work which the student could be put onto writing up as his own thesis. Something of this kind has been happening for a long time in certain research groups, especially those in high energy physics. But the procedure raises certain problems that will grow larger as group research extends more widely, and it may not be easy simply to brush them under the mat.

One difficulty I met lies in the fact that the detailed way in which this kind of approach is made can vary from department to department, with some straining at a gnat while others swallow a camel. And this reflects a wider problem — that certain usages have grown up which stretch the spirit, if not the letter, of what is intended by a PhD, without their validity or their implications for what can broadly be described as the standard of the PhD ever being adequately considered.

What is happening, in effect, is a marked deviation from the examination for the PhD as it is generally known and accepted. Normally the student shows, by the results of his work, that he is capable of planning and carrying to success a sustained programme of research: by his thesis he shows that he is also capable of describing his research in a coherent way and relating his findings to knowledge and theory in his field.

The student taking part in group research, however, is still, at the end of three years, at an early stage of learning the more complex task of planning, sustaining and carrying through major research. If he is given a small part of the joint enterprise to plan, carry out with the help of others, and write up as a thesis, all perhaps in the last few months of his three years, though his training may be far better, and he may have acquired a range of highly useful skills, the work he is presenting to the examiners seems unlikely to be comparable with the product of a student who has reported the results of all his three years' work. In such cases, the internal examiner is, presumably, aware of the general calibre of the student's work and is judging him as much on that as on the thesis, while the external examiner knows, and is influenced by, the quality of the work of the group as a whole, and accepts the internal examiner's judgement of that part of the student's work that is not to be seen. This is where the element of pretence comes in that was referred to by the Working Party.

I am sure that justice is, in general, done; but I am less sure that it can be seen to be done. It seems to me there is a strong case for universities to look rather carefully at the question of what kind of thesis can be expected of students taking part in group research, and the other ways in which their competence can be judged — if only to maintain some kind of parity between different research groups.

Rising Expectations
Outside group research, too, the Swinnerton-Dyer Working Party seem to have felt that there was nothing wrong with the form and nature of the PhD in the natural sciences. They say of this: 'It is generally accepted that the yardstick of a satisfactory PhD thesis is the amount of research that a competent and reasonably diligent candidate can be expected to do in three years'.

Regrettably, they seem to have been unaware of the tendency for the amount expected of a PhD student to grow. In the natural sciences, over the last quarter of a century alone, what is expected of the 'competent and reasonably diligent candidate' has changed from what he can do in two years, write up in the succeeding nine months, and submit comfortably within his third year. It is now what he can do over three years and write up over a longer period.

There is a similar, but perhaps worse, problem of changing expectations in the arts and social sciences. In the natural sciences the student knows he must finish his experimentation, or whatever he is doing, before he leaves the university at the end of the three years. In the arts and social sciences, there is no such clear point of termination to any part of the work.

For the social sciences, the Working Party seem to have accepted what I would regard as a rather specious argument, that the natural size for a piece of research is a book – after all, research theses are written for the MPhil, and these are shorter than for the PhD. They are shorter still for an MA, and even the work for a bachelors degree can, on occasions, result in a minor piece of publishable research. Perhaps what is not book-length is being defined as not research in the same way that what Jowett did not know was not knowledge.

I say they *seem* to have accepted this argument, for, though they also accept that writing a book is likely to take more than three years, the Working Party go on to say that there is a need in the social sciences for a degree to be completed in three years and to include an adequate training in research. It can be called either a PhD or by some other name, they care not which.

I would not for a moment wish to disagree with their conclusion, though I dislike their path to it. It is unsatisfactory that PhDs should know only the latest fashion in their branch of the social sciences, which may, by itself, contribute only a little to the understanding of a narrow range of problems. However, to introduce a new degree without some realization that the pressure towards the raising of expectations about what a doctoral candidate must achieve could affect this new degree too, is to invite future problems.

One possibility might be, in all fields together, somehow to reverse the trend and reduce the time a PhD is expected to take – I imagine that that is what the Working Party was, perhaps subconsciously, seeking to do in its proposal for the social sciences. It is certainly worth trying, but I am sceptical about the chances of success. That is why I put forward the above suggestion that the current level of the PhD be accepted, but the period of part-time work on it be transferred from the end to the beginning. It is an essential part of my suggestion that all the remaining stages, even including, perhaps, the examination, would be completed within the three years of full-time study.

There would still be the problem of how to keep that work firmly within the three years and stop it creeping over and beyond. One hope of an answer would seem to come from departments of economics, who, I am told, have got together and agreed ways of holding standards for PhDs. Probably the main hope for holding the level would come from the working downwards of the pressures for higher completion rates, applied by the award-granting bodies, together with an awareness in the universities that over-ambitious projects lower the completion rates.

I said above that there is still room for improvement in the training of PhD students in the techniques needed for their research. But what about their training in other techniques used in their subject but irrelevant to their topics? Is it only in the social sciences that there is a need to train students in a wider range of techniques for research? Should there not, perhaps, be some intermediate examination in research techniques that students have to pass before being allowed to submit a PhD thesis?

A Case for a Thorough Review
I have raised here a number of issues relating to the form and structure of the MPhil and the PhD. These are.

1 The need to ensure that all the students receive a wide training in research, perhaps enforcing this by requiring them to pass an intermediate examination.
2 The need to standardize the level of these degrees so that it is, as nearly as possible, the same in every subject and field of study.
3 The need to hold the levels of these degrees steady so that the effort required to pass stops rising.
4 The possibility of extending the procedures by which the candidates for the PhD can submit published work instead of a thesis.
5 The need to reach overall agreement on a suitable way of examining candidates who have taken part in group research, and to ensure that this is generally adopted.
6 The need to provide an effective machinery for appeals against examiners' decisions.

The PhD was originally introduced into Britain by all the universities of the day acting virtually in unison. Some measure of this uniformity still survives, fostered by the use of external examiners. It has its value, and, if it is to continue, the universities need to act together now in considering possible changes. Indeed, any changes today would need to involve also the Council for National Academic Awards.

Therefore I strongly urge the universities, acting through the Committee of Vice-Chancellors, and together with the CNAA, to set up a commission to review the structure of research degrees in Britain.

References

Advisory Board for the Research Councils (ABRC) (1982) *Report of the Working Party on Postgraduate Education (Swinnerton-Dyer Report) Cmnd.8537* London: HMSO

Berelson, B. (1960) *Graduate Education in the United States* New York, Toronto & London: McGraw-Hill Book Co.

Bligh, D. (1981) Doctoring the figures *The Times Higher Education Supplement* 430 (30.1.1981)p.12

Brown, C. (1982) *The Education and Employment of Postgraduates* London: Policy Studies Institute

Cartter, A.M. (1976) *PhDs and the Academic Labor Market* New York, Toronto & London: McGraw-Hill Book Co.

Christopherson, Sir D. et al. (1982) *Research Student and Supervisor: a Discussion Document on Good Supervisory Practice* Swindon: Science and Engineering Research Council

Davis, J.A. (1962) *Stipends and Spouses: the Finances of American Arts and Sciences Graduate Students* Chicago and London: University of Chicago Press

Economic and Social Research Council (ESRC) (1984a) Research theses submission rates: Latest survey results *Newsletter 52* London: ESRC

Economic and Social Research Council (ESRC) (1984b) *The Preparation and Supervision of Research Theses in the Social Sciences* London: ESRC

Gilbert, Sir W.S. (1878) *HMS Pinafore*

Glennester, H. (1966) *Graduate School: a Study of Graduate Work at the London School of Economics* Edinburgh and London: Oliver and Boyd

Katz, J. and Hartnett, R.T. (Eds) (1976). *Scholars in the Making: the Development of Graduate and Professional Students* Cambridge, Mass.: Ballinger Publishing Co.

Joint SERC-SSRC Committee (1983) *Interdisciplinary Research: Selection, Supervision and Training* Swindon and London: SERC and SSRC

Kelsall, R.K., Poole, A. and Kuhn, A. (1972) *Graduates: the Sociology of the Elite* London: Methuen and Co.

Krebs, Sir H. (1967) The making of a scientist *Nature* 215, 1441-5

Political and Economic Planning (PEP) (1956) *Graduate Employment: a Sample Survey* London: George Allen and Unwin

Rudd, E. and Hatch, S.R. (1968) *Graduate Study and After* London: Weidenfeld and Nicolson

Rudd, E. (1975) *The Highest Education* London and Boston: Routledge and Kegan Paul

Rudd, E. (1980) Halls of residence for students: a cautionary tale of decision-making *The Political Quarterly* 51, 164-174

Rudd, E. (1983) How not to do policy research *The Times Higher Education Supplement* 539 (4.3.1983)

Rudd, E. (1984) Research into postgraduate education *Higher Education Research and Development* 3(2)109–20.

Science and Engineering Research Council (SERC) (1984) PhD submission rates: studentship awards beginning in 1979 *SERC Bulletin* 2(11) 27

Solmon, L.C., Kent, L., Ochsner, N.L. and Hurwicz, M-L. (1981) *Underemployed PhDs* Lexington and Toronto: Lexington Books

Welsh, J.M. (1978) The supervision of postgraduate research students *Research in Education* 19, 77-86

Welsh, J.M. (1979) *The First Year of Postgraduate Research Study* Guildford: SRHE

Welsh, J.M. (1980a) Predicting postgraduate performance *Notes of University Teaching 1* University Teaching Centre, University of Aberdeen

Welsh, J.M. (1980b) *The Postgraduate Student: Progress and Problems* PhD thesis, University of Aberdeen

Welsh, J.M. (1981a) Improving the supervision of postgraduate students *Research in Education*

Welsh, J.M. (1981b) Writing and the PhD student *Journal of Georgraphy in Higher Education* 5(2) 212-4

Welsh, J.M. (1981c) The PhD student at work *Studies in Higher Education* 6(2) 159-62

Whalley, A. (1982) *Postgraduate Education in Universities and Polytechnics* London: Policy Studies Institute

Williamson, P. (1981) *Early Careers of 1970 Graduates* London: Department of Employment Unit for Manpower Studies, Research Paper 26

Index

The Society for Research into Higher Education

The Society for Research into Higher Education exists to encourage and co-ordinate research and development in all aspects of higher education. It thus draws to public attention both the need for research and development and the needs of the research community. Its income is derived from subscriptions, and from research or other specific grants. It is wholly independent. Its corporate members are universities, polytechnics, institutes of higher education, research institutions and professional and governmental bodies. Its individual members are teachers and researchers, administrators and students. Members are found in all parts of the world and the Society regards its international work as amongst its most important activities.

The Society discusses and comments on policy, organizes conferences and sponsors research. Under the imprint SRHE & NFER-NELSON it is a specialist publisher of research, having over 30 titles in print. It also publishes Studies in Higher Education *(three times a year),* Higher Education Abstracts *(three times a year),* International Newsletter *(twice a year), a* Bulletin *(six times a year), and jointly with the Committee for Research into Teacher Education (CRITE)* Evaluation Newsletter *(twice a year).*

The Society's committees, study groups and local branches are run by members, with help from a small secretariat, and aim to provide a forum for discussion. Some of the groups, at present the Teacher Education Study Group and the Staff Development Group, have their own subscriptions and organization, as do some Regional Branches. The Governing Council, elected by members, comments on current issues and discusses policies with leading figures in politics and education. The Society organizes seminars on current research for officials of the DES and other ministries, and is in touch with bodies in Britain such as the CNAA, NAB, CVCP, UGC and the British Council; and with sister-bodies overseas. Its current research projects include one on the relationship between entry qualifications and degree results, directed by Prof. W.D. Furneaux (Brunel) and one on 'Questions of Quality' directed by Prof. G.C. Moodie (York).

The Society's annual conferences take up central themes, viz. 'Education for the Professions' (1984, with the help and support of DTI, UNESCO and many professional bodies), 'Continuing Education' (1985, organized in collaboration with Goldsmiths' College, the Open University and the University of Surrey, with advice from the DES and the CBI), 'Standards and criteria in HE' (1986). Joint conferences are held, viz. 'Cognitive Processes' (1985, with the Cognitive Psychology Section of the BPS), on the DES 'Green Paper' (1985, with The Times Higher Education Supplement*) and on 'Information Technology' (1986, with the Council for Educational Technology). For some of the Society's conferences, special studies are commissioned in advance, as 'Precedings'.*

Members receive free of charge the Society's Abstracts, *annual conference proceedings (or 'Precedings'), and* Bulletin *and* International Newsletter, *and may buy SRHE & NFER-NELSON books at booksellers' discount. Corporate members receive the Society's journal* Studies in Higher Education *free, individuals at a heavy discount. They may also obtain* Evaluation Newsletter *and certain other journals at discount, including the NFER* Register of Educational Research.

Further information may be obtained from the Society for Research into Higher Education, At the University, Guildford GU2 5XH, UK.